MAKE YOUR KIDS
SMARTER

Also by Erika V. Shearin Karres, Ed.D.

Violence Proof Your Kids Now

MAKE YOUR KIDS
SMA⁺RTER

50 TOP TEACHER TIPS FOR GRADES K TO 8

Erika V. Shearin Karres, Ed. D.

**Andrews McMeel
Publishing**

Kansas City

Book design by Pete Lippincott

02 03 04 05 06 MVP 10 9 8 7 6 5 4 3 2 1

Library of Congress Cataloging-in-Publication Data

Karres, Erika V. Shearin.
    Make your kids smarter : 50 top teacher tips for grades K to 8 / Erika V. Shearin Karres.
        p. cm.
    Includes bibliographical references (p.).
    ISBN 0-7407-2207-7
    1. Education—Parent participation—Handbooks, manuals, etc. 2. Home and school—Handbooks, manuals, etc.
    3. Academic achievement—Handbooks, manuals, etc.
    I. Title.

LB1048.5.K37 2001
371.3'028'1—dc21
                                                    2001053755

ATTENTION: SCHOOLS AND BUSINESSES

Andrews McMeel books are available at quantity discounts with bulk purchase for educational, business, or sales promotional use. For information, please write to: Special Sales Department, Andrews McMeel Publishing, 4520 Main Street, Kansas City, Missouri 64111.

Knowledge is power.

—HOBBES, *LEVIATHAN*

Knowledge is the only instrument of production that is not subject to diminishing returns.

—J. M. CLARK, *JOURNAL OF POLITICAL ECONOMY*

When books are opened, you discover you have wings.

—HELEN HAYES

This book is for my daughters,
Elizabeth Shearin Hounshell and Dr. Mary D. Shearin,
and my husband, Andrew Matthew Karres,
and my granddaughters,
Katie Hounshell and Sarah Hounshell.

Contents

Prologue

Every child is born a potential genius.
    —R. BUCKMINSTER FULLER

CONGRATULATIONS! What a wonderful parent you are! How can I tell? You picked up this book, so I know you truly care about your kids and want them to thrive; you're not just saying this, you really mean it.

Indeed, you're not only willing to give your kids the best environment in which to grow, you want to give them an extra-special something that will make them surge ahead and experience success now and later on. That extra something is a few more minutes of your day.

Let's face it. In these hectic times the lives of all of us are too busy, complex, and stressful. In the majority of families, both parents work, if there *are* two parents. And if there is only one, the sole breadwinner does double or triple duty. In either case, there is precious little time left for the kids.

But you, special parent that you are, will manage to find those extra minutes. For you realize that in the midst of your harried lifestyle, one thing fortunately is a constant. No matter how thin you're stretched or how crazy your schedule gets, you know what's most important: your kids.

Oh, yes, our kids are at the center of our existence. No matter how we have to scramble, we want them to strive and thrive, to grow up to live good, productive lives—in other words, to be successful.

Yet while we all ardently wish and work for that, we already know that the road to success can be tricky. Our children's lives aren't a bed of roses either. Kids today face many more pressures than we did, both in and out of school. As a consequence, we tend to fret and worry. We know our kids are fine for the moment, but what about the days to come? Will they prosper the way we want them to? How can we make sure, in the little spare time we have, that we don't overlook our children's needs? What can we do to give them an edge in their daily lives, lives that revolve so heavily around school—whether it's preschool or elementary, middle, or beyond? What can we add on—easily and quickly—to enhance their true potential, rev up their academic skills and school savvy, and make them just a little more competitive as they climb the scholastic ladder?

As devoted parents, we want our kids to have the best school tools we can give them to send them on their journey, to let them feel better about themselves, and to truly enable them to spread their wings and soar—all in just a few minutes a week.

Even those parents who have more quality time to spend with their kids feel that way. They too want to equip their offspring with every possible advantage they can.

But is that possible? Yes. And how is it possible? By using this book.

Make Your Kids Smarter: 50 Top Teacher Tips for Grades K to 8 provides—assembled in one handy volume—every school tool, skill, and drill needed to give your kids the upper hand. Rest assured that with the help of this book you can supply them with many tried-and-true brain gainers and state-of-the-art school smarts to "failure-proof" them.

You do this first by quickly checking where they stand at present. Then you add to their knowledge with basic common-sense gap fillers or quick skill builders here and there—or, if you so desire, even more advanced tools and tasks. It's all up to you; you choose.

This book will walk you through the process of making your kids smarter step by step, with simple Parent Pointers, FYI explanations and guided mini lessons, all gathered right from the best source—the classrooms of thousands of the country's top teachers. All these professionals say that the early school grades are the prime time for learning. That means you must make use of those important early years. They really are the best time to prepare and potentiate your kids' minds.

That's it. In this one small volume you have a one-stop school-skill resource for your kids. Not only is it easy to access, but it will be a lasting reference for you throughout your children's schooling. For the tips span the whole spectrum of what kids need to know these days, from the commonsensical to the more technical—all right at your fingertips and just waiting for you to use whenever and wherever you feel like it, in whatever way is comfortable *for you*.

And being the involved parent that you are, you can do it. You *will* do it.

How quickly you'll see the results. In just a few minutes every week you'll power up your kids' potential, sharpen their skills, help them stay ahead of the game, and make their lives easier. That will surely make your life easier too. Most important, it will make your kids quicker and better, both academically and in their hearts.

Let's be honest: Today's schools aren't all first-rate, no matter how much we wish they were. Some kids, through no fault of their own, find themselves in a bleak educational environment. Never mind how hard their teachers work, sometimes those students don't have a chance to learn even the basics in a timely fashion. That means when they're old enough to enter middle school, their skills will be one or more grades behind.

This is only one of the conditions this book addresses, to give parents and caregivers some "education insurance" and peace of mind. For all the basic *underlying* skills kids really need to know in elementary and middle school are encapsulated here. That means their teachers can then concentrate on just the specifics that remain unlearned.

There's nothing more important to a child than to succeed in school. I know, because I have spent all my working years in classrooms. And up to now, there has been no book like *Make Your Kids Smarter*. Sure, there are lots of books on education, but most of them are written from the point of view of either a college professor, a child psychologist, or an academic drill- and taskmaster. Not a single one incorporates the cumulative experience of a veteran public school teacher and educator who has collected school tools, learning tips, quips, and quick tricks for over thirty-five years, tried and perfected on tens of thousands of students and parents.

I know school skills inside out and understand how important improving them is to your kids' future.

In talking with hundreds—no, thousands—of other teachers, I have heard them say the same thing over and over: Kids who do well in school are on a roll, a roll toward success in life. For the success we experience in school usually translates into the success we experience in life. School is where it all starts.

As you go through this book, you will notice that a majority of the top teacher tips deal with increasing your kids' language abilities: reading, writing, listening, and speaking. Math and science are hardly mentioned. This book isn't about specific subjects; it's a devoted to general skills. So why the heavy emphasis on reading and writing?

Because reading and writing are needed to do better in *all* subjects. Good language skills almost guarantee improved grades in everything kids study in school. That's why you want to upgrade your kids' reading and writing tools. The more those skills are reinforced, the better they stick.

Another reason? In a society that's getting ever more complex, a good command of language is the most important tool for success. "The limits of my language mean the limits of my world," said Ludwig Wittgenstein. We want to give our kids the whole wide world, not just a tiny slice of it, right?

User's Manual

THE BEST WAY for parents and other adults to make use of these top teacher tips is to be flexible. First, look at your schedule for each day, for each week, for each month. Ask yourself, Where can I find a few more minutes? I know how busy you are. These days all parents and caregivers are busy, and those with kids from kindergarten through eighth grade are especially harried. But surely there are a few minutes each day, each week, that you can use.

How about when you are stuck in traffic taking the kids to school? (According to a recent study, Americans spend an average of thirty-six hours a year stuck in traffic.) Or when you are waiting for soccer practice to end so you can chauffeur your kids home? That's a good time to refresh your own memory in the FYI sections. Then, on the drive home, you can ask your children some pertinent questions. Drill them in a skill.

As you drop your older daughter off for her ballet or piano lesson and have to while away an hour anyway—going home doesn't make sense for that short a time—you and the younger kids can attack a few facts.

How about a rainy weekend when everyone's stuck inside? Or on a trip to visit the grandparents: While one parent is driving, the other can start a word game. There are so many "Make Your Kids Smarter" moments.

Maybe your kids are home with a slight cold, not well enough to go to school but well enough to learn a little something.

How about when you're waiting at the doctor's or dentist's for the nurse to call you and your child? That's fifteen or twenty empty minutes right there—empty until you use that time to make some scholastic progress.

So much time is spent waiting with our kids for the pediatrician, the orthodontist, the optometrist: yearly checkups and shots, colds and flu that spread like wildfire, braces, glasses, or contact lenses. Now we can make use of every single waiting moment.

Please be flexible with your time—and be creative. Play games with your kids and weave in some of these learning drills. Late afternoon, when you toss a ball to them, also toss out a brain-gaining question. Have them name a part of speech. When they rake leaves, have them rake their minds as well for definitions of difficult words. When you tuck a love-you note into a nutritious lunch, tuck in some extra nutrition for their brain, maybe by writing *What's the plural of hippopotamus?* on the back of the note. That evening over supper, ask your kids what they found out.

You can drop this book into your purse or pocket or keep it stashed in your car's glove compartment, or under the front seat of the van. Keep it at the office to flip through at lunch. Have it on hand for whenever there's a free second.

Think for a moment of all the examples of when you could better use your time. What about the annual camping trip? The flight out to Arizona to see the grandparents? The great trip to the beach every summer? Sooner or later the kids will be ready to come in from a long day at the ocean . . . and you can be ready with a quick word, a light lesson, a hug and a scholastic hint, a terrific quick teaching tip.

And what a special bonding time this can be. Nothing cements parents and kids more than a shared quest for school success. And that's what this book is all about. Getting smarter will excite and inspire your kids. As they catch on to all the little school tricks of the trade, as they learn top teacher tips from you, as they think more and absorb more knowledge, they will be so thrilled. Just as I am to be able to help you get started on this exciting journey.

This is the format.

To start, take just a couple of minutes a day, no more than fifteen minutes a week, to go over a tip or two. In no time you will notice your daughter doing better in school, your son coming home challenged by his day. Don't be surprised if your kids clamor for more learning time with you. After all, you are their first and best teacher, their finest study buddy. If you take the time and make the effort to help your kids climb the academic ladder, they will scramble up faster than ever before and ask for more hints on how they can do even better.

This book is arranged by related areas, so if your child has already conquered one topic, go on to the next or skip around according to his or her school-related weaknesses, interests detected, or special strengths.

The Parent Pointers are meant for you, Mom, Dad, and Caregiver. In them I address the tip or tool about to be covered. Sometimes I give you a reason for it; other times I provide a focus or context; still other times, I throw out a question or two for you to ponder.

The FYI segment contains definitions and explanations. Every so often in this section, I may also refresh your memory. Parents and caregivers will remember much of what they learned in elementary and middle school, but some items may have faded over the years, and a quick review can come in handy.

Also, some scholastic skills may be different from the way we learned them when we went to school. Other skills may not have been needed until high school, but as the pace of the world has been speeding up, so have the demands made on our kids. Often what we learned later, they now have to study sooner.

Today, because of an increased emphasis on achievement testing and state exams, the educational content areas for the various grades may be quite different from what you remember. It's a rare school system that isn't embroiled year after year in some sort of school reform—expectation raising, curriculum revamping—and in the ever-toughening academic requirements for college.

This isn't the charming era of the little red schoolhouse anymore. School change is an ever-present reality. And as part of that change, our kids are being asked to perform better and better.

The Helpful How-to Hints are the meat of this book. They present what must be gone over with your kids: taught, reviewed, remembered. Think of the hints as steps to your goal of making your kids smarter. Again, you need to be flexible and creative here, to deal quickly with some of the hints while lingering over others. It all depends on your situation. You know best what your child already knows, which gaps need filling, and which of the two levels of school skills presented here is appropriate.

The Smart Starter exercises and suggestions are for a younger child or for one just getting into the academic swing of things: kids in the earlier grades, or those who haven't liked school up to now and are lagging behind, or those who attended a school not known for high achievement scores; also, all those kids whose grades haven't matched their true talents so far—which is any and all kids who bring home grades lower than B.

The Super Starter exercises and suggestions are for kids who may be older, or are in the higher grades, are already making B's and the occasional A but could still do better; also, all those kids who are just plain ready for advanced work. You'll find out soon enough where each child belongs, once you've checked out what your kids really know.

This book is also a good record of your time spent assisting your kids with schoolwork. Most teachers are adamant about one thing: They do not want parents to do their kids' homework for them. But they would give anything if the parents would shore up their kids' study skills, pique their interest in scholastics, and help them think. And that's exactly what you're going to do.

The blank Notes & Quotes section at the end of each chapter is your scholastic-parenting journal. Here is where you can jot down brief comments, dates, thoughts, and reflections as you go through this book. You can record when you worked on this skill and on that school tool. What was simple or complex about it. What worked, what didn't. Where more help is needed.

And as you pass on the learning tips to your kids, please listen to them carefully. That's *most* important. Write down their comments, their quotes. If they say, "That's easy, Dad" or "Mom, I know that already"—that's what you want to note: for further reference, to use later in the school year, to refresh their memory and yours, to mark off as a drill done, or to apply with younger kids or those you baby-sit regularly or look after once in a while.

How do you start? Just turn the page. The first section is the most important one. Top teachers everywhere agree that the most important school skill students of any age need is the skill of listening well. So, we'll begin with that.

Part I: School Smarts

Help your kids to . . .
become the best listeners possible

You are now embarking on a terrific adventure. How exciting to help your kids tackle those school skills that will bring enormous benefits to them.

1 | Be a Good Listener

PARENT POINTER *Teach your kids to listen carefully to their teachers.*

It is said that roughly 75 percent of all school instruction is delivered through oral communication. And in the workplace people devote over 33 percent of their working hours to face-to-face talking. Even in this era of sophisticated electronic communication devices, oral language is what counts. So children really have to learn to listen—and listen well.

As we all know, kids are self-centered. That is normal; it exists from birth on. It's what makes them survive and grow—their concentration on themselves, their focus on the *me*.

As they grow older, children do move away from their constant emphasis on me-me-me and learn to relate to others: moms and dads, their caregivers, and their peers. This process isn't always smooth and takes longer for some kids than for others. But by the time they enter kindergarten, most youngsters have learned to shift their constant focus away from their own needs and onto adults, their teachers.

They learn to listen.

FYI

What can get in the way is TV.

For many kids, TV has become a second parent. Yet, unlike a human being, TV is never dull or demanding. It is always filled with changing images, vivid music, funny things, enticing messages. If not—*click!* You just turn it off.

Plus TV never tells you stuff to do, right?

That's why a teacher's job is so much harder these days, especially in elementary and middle school. Teachers have to get the kids to focus on them, not blandly, like observers, but actively, as respondents. Teachers inform and direct and ask for results.

Of course, kids nowadays also spend a lot of time on video games and computer activities. But again, the big difference here is that those toys react *to* the wishes of the kids. Techno gadgets can be manipulated, played with, made to conform to the kids' directions. They can be mastered or shut off. Teachers cannot. They have a set of expectations and lesson plans to carry out.

This presents a major conflict for the TV-reared child. In school, the vid kid has to play the role of a follower, a learner: a *student.* And the plan of action, the classroom "menu," isn't one of choice. It's posted on the chalkboard and won't respond to the remote.

Obviously, a switch has to be made from what the child wants to what the teacher wants. That's where most school problems occur if kids haven't learned the most basic school skill, and that is to really listen to the teacher. Once that is accomplished, everything else is easy.

But how is that done?

HELPFUL HOW-TO HINTS

First, test your kids on this important skill. Do they listen to you? When you tell them to pick up their toys and come to supper, do they comply fairly quickly? When you say it's time for homework, do your kids get their books out?

Or do you have to remind them over and over before you get results? Do you have to resort to the old "one-two-three or else!" threat more than once a week to get them to get ready for bed?

If your kids listen to you at home, you can count on their listening in school. If not, here's what you do.

SMART STARTER Speak correctly and clearly to your child, and expect results. It does no good to mumble and then have to repeat yourself. If you're tempted to curse, don't. Jason doesn't know any better than to imitate you.

Model good listening skills. Pay close attention to Jason when *he* talks to *you*. Answer him when he asks a question. Don't ignore him, no matter how many questions he has.

Explain to him the importance of being a good listener and then test him. While he's watching TV, walk into the kitchen and say, "Jason, come here a minute." Then count the seconds it takes for him to show up. Tell him *twenty seconds*, if that's how long it took, and record it on a sheet of paper that you post on the fridge. Later, when you tell him it's time for homework, again notice how long it takes him to open his books. Same goes for bedtime. Next day, tell Jason that from now on whenever he takes more than five seconds to get moving, it will affect his bedtime: one minute earlier to bed for every second he dawdles over the five-second limit. Kids dislike having to go to bed early. In no time, Jason's listening skills should improve drastically.

Be sure to praise him for any improvements he makes in listening, even if it takes a while. Praise has a positive effect on behavior.

Finally, turn off the TV whenever possible and read to Jason; then have him read to you. Discuss what was read and have him retell the story.

SUPER STARTER With an older child, or one with ingrained bad listening habits, begin at school. Ask Jennifer's teachers how well she responds to directions. Also, does she talk when she's not supposed to? Does she have to be reminded to open her book? To begin working? Then make note of the teachers' replies. If all is well, over half the battle is won. Some kids do develop good listening skills at school but refuse to listen at home. In that case, you need a system similar to the one suggested for Jason.

Discuss the problem with Jennifer, establish a system of consequences for not listening to you, and stick to them. Three weeks of enforcing the new plan usually does the trick.

But what if Jennifer listens neither at home nor in school? Then work with her teachers on a plan of rewards and reckonings. Get advice from the guidance counselor as well. And get help from the Internet sources listed in the back of this book.

Be consistent in sticking to the plan you have set up with the teacher, and don't back down. This is the most important school skill to work on. Kids who listen well to their parents and teachers *always* do better in school than those who don't. They're almost failure-proof.

Notes & Quotes

_____

_____

_____

_____

_____

Just imagine if your children could only absorb half the nutrients from what they ate. That would worry you. You'd think, My kids are starving! Well, school transmits brain food. If your kids aren't listening well, they only get a fraction of what they need to be successful in class. In other words, they'll end up achievement-starved.

Same goes for the home. If they tune you out regularly, only a very few child-rearing comments you make on a daily basis ever penetrate. Think about it: The most important lessons you want to teach—those about life—may never reach them. So, please get their listening skills up to par. Make it happen, beginning today, and praise them freely for their efforts.

Good listening skills, however, are easier to come by in an environment where children feel comfortable: safe and well liked. We all listen better if we feel secure and sure. Let's work on that next.

2 | Know Your Way Around School

PARENT POINTER *Help your kids to be familiar with their school.*

Children spend seven or eight hours a day in what was formerly the little red schoolhouse. After their home, the school building, grounds, and staff are their most important environment. And when you discount the time kids spend sleeping and add in all the hours they are occupied with school-related activities, enrichment classes, tutoring sessions, and sporting events, it's easy to see that school can seem more important than the home.

Ask yourself, How well do I know my kids' school and the teachers who work there?

FYI

Many schools today are huge buildings, some several stories high, with enormous grounds, vast hallways, meandering walkways, and impressive sports facilities. Today's school complex can look like a mini college campus.

Or it can look like an aging high-rise with narrow halls, sagging staircases, windowless dusty rooms, leaky roofs, and spooky corners.

But no matter whether schools are dreamboats or dinosaurs, they can be confusing to our kids. And scary. So please, really introduce your kids to their school and grounds in such a manner that they know the structures as well as their own homes.

HELPFUL HOW-TO HINTS

SMART STARTER Before the school year begins, take your kids for an extended walk through the buildings and grounds. Discuss what impresses you favorably. Keep any critical remarks to yourself.

In addition to your children's teachers, meet the principal, assistant principal, secretary, librarian, guidance counselor, and cafeteria staff and talk with them. Do that *in addition* to the cursory introduction you will receive at the back-to-school open house.

At home, have Shanika draw a sketch of her school on a sheet of paper and fill in the names of the teachers and programs she knows. Have her draw the way she walks—to class, to the library, to the rest room, to the cafeteria. Ask her if there is any area of the school complex she doesn't know. If there is, introduce her to the parts she's not familiar with.

Ask Shanika what she would do if she had an emergency, such as forgetting her lunch money, losing a book, or getting sick. Then help her come up with a plan. Discuss how she could phone you, and make sure that she and the office have an alternate number—perhaps another family member—at hand. Explain that you will come and get her if she's sick and where she should wait for you. Have a practice run, if possible.

Go over the school handbook with Shanika and make sure she understands all the rules. Of course, her teacher will do that too, but think of the advantages if you have laid the groundwork. Remember, it takes several times for all of us to learn something new, but it takes kids even longer.

Also, volunteer at school as much as possible. Perhaps you can:

1. Offer to help the teacher in the classroom one or more hours a month.

2. Help with the preparation of new units or worksheets, and use some of your time at home researching new materials and exercises via the Internet.

3. Ask the teacher for a wish list of supplies and other extras, then write a check and send it in to be used for those extra supplies (volunteering by proxy).

All three methods of volunteering, by strengthening the bond between your kids and the school, will make them want to listen even more carefully to their teachers.

SUPER STARTER But what about your son Shawn, who already knows more than you about his school since he's been in the same building, though in different rooms, for several years now?

Ask him about all the teachers and other staff and about school rules, library rules, and regulations.

Ask him about extracurricular activities. Have him check out two or three clubs and report back to you with his picks and pans. Urge him to join at least one club or go out for one sports team.

Ask him to draw or describe his dream school, compare it to the real school he is attending, and see if there is anything Shawn and his classmates can do to make some improvement.

Join the PTA, start a beautification committee, and get Shawn, some other parents, and their kids to join in a spruce-up campaign.

Ask Shawn what he would do if there was a problem at school. Make sure he can reach you, or another adult whom you have designated as your backup parent, at all times. Discuss school violence with him and explain that telling you and his teacher of anything harmful he's observing is doing the school and the students a favor. Also discuss this topic with his teacher. Is there a way kids can notify the administration about something bad going on they have observed without their classmates' knowledge? Does the school have a resource officer? Is there a suggestion box? A helping hotline? Only when adults know about a potential problem can they help a troubled kid or stop detrimental behaviors. Have a similar conversation about these topics frequently with Shawn. Talking once or twice a year about potential dangers kids face at school isn't enough these days.

Notes & Quotes

_____

_____

_____

_____

_____

It's time for a compliment, and this one's for you: Well done. In times past, we didn't have to worry about our kids being safe in school, but nowadays this is a necessity. You must do all you can to ensure that your kids feel truly at home and safe there. Only then can they concentrate on learning.

Once kids are able to really listen, they need to learn to focus from the moment they enter the classroom, since these days most teachers cram all sorts of materials into their presentation and try to use every minute for instruction.

If kids waste time and stare out the window for the first few minutes, they might miss some of the most important parts of the lesson at hand, simply by not paying attention to the teacher.

3 | Pay Attention

PARENT POINTER *Teach your kids to pay attention from the moment they enter the classroom.*

Do you ever forget things? Has your mate asked you to do something, and a second later you can't remember what it was? Most likely the reason was that your mind was on something else; your brain was on overload.

FYI

The same can happen with your kids. They are often on information overload as well. Plus, as TV-reared or TV-influenced youngsters, they have been trained to have short attention spans.

Additionally, there is often so much noise in school hallways, such a rumble in the cafeteria, and so many other kids all dying to talk to them that the school resembles an enormous mall, filled with throngs of excited students all shouting at one another.

So kids are often in a daze. But they must learn to pay attention from the moment they enter their classroom.

HELPFUL HOW-TO HINTS

SMART STARTER Buy Alfredo a small notebook and have him fill in the days of the week. Show him how to list each date and write under it the various subjects he has, such as reading or arithmetic, leaving space under each subject. Tell him from now on to copy the pages or assignments written on the chalkboard as soon as he enters the classroom each day.

Ask for that notebook every evening and read the information that was copied. It doesn't have to be neat, but it has to be understandable. Then help Alfredo check off the homework assignments according to what's listed in the notebook, after they have been completed. In this manner you can keep up with what Alfredo is doing every day. Just look at the notebook, check his homework, and cross off the items together. Or help him study for the upcoming spelling test. When the notepad looks ragged, get another one but save the old one for a reference.

SUPER STARTER With an older child, check the assignment notebook only once a week or if there is a problem. For instance, if Allegra keeps forgetting about a test or a project that's due and you and she have to scramble around collecting stuff at the last minute, that's a red flag. In that case, you need to glance at her notebook every day. You'll soon find out that the science project was assigned three weeks ago. Or that the suddenly remembered book report was posted as homework last month.

Then take the next step. Teach Allegra to copy daily assignments, chapters to be reviewed, and upcoming history test dates into her notebook, and to circle the major long-term assignments and huge deadlines. Then show her how to transfer the big assignment dates onto a master calendar you keep at home, prominently displayed on the fridge or the kitchen wall.

Instead of recording only the final due dates, help Allegra set some mini deadlines. Have her list half the pages to be read for a book report, or the rough draft for an essay, two weeks before the actual due date. In the case of a science fair presentation, have her split up the task into four smaller jobs: choosing the topic, making a rough outline, gathering information on note cards, and completing the project. Each of the smaller jobs deserves its own deadline! School assignments are like getting ready for a major holiday. You can't wait until Thanksgiving Day when your dinner guests are pulling into the driveway to buy the turkey and cranberry sauce.

Also confer with Allegra's teachers and find out if she's paying attention during class and is prepared for school. Sometimes a change in seating arrangements is required to move your child up front, so she can see all the reminders and assignments posted on the chalkboard.

Notes & Quotes

_____

_____

_____

_____

_____

_____

Your kids now have the necessary background to become smarter. But don't expect perfection, only improvement, and, as always, be sure to say, I'm so glad you're doing better. I'm so happy you're trying, really trying, to pay attention!

Some people attribute the passivity many youngsters exhibit these days to constant TV watching. Others see it as a normal part of their development. Whatever the reason, too many kids nowadays only go through the motions of paying attention in class. Maybe they have learned to be quiet and sit still at their desks. And they will copy down assignments and hand in their work obediently the next day. But they're missing out on a most important skill, and that is the ability to speak up in class and ask questions.

4 | Ask Questions

PARENT POINTER *Teach your kids to ask questions.*

Have you ever gone to your doctor for a checkup and then later said to yourself, I wish I had asked about such-and-such? Or have you attended a meeting or class, only to have five unanswered questions pop up in your mind after the meeting was over? If you had only asked them while the session was in progress, think of how much time and energy you might have saved yourself.

The same thing can happen in school.

Thus, the next learning tip is very important. Without it, even the smartest kids can't reach their potential. That skill is to overcome being shy, to speak up and ask questions in class.

FYI

Most kids hate being embarrassed. When teachers keep them after class, kids often have no problem asking about something they didn't understand during a lesson but never even mention until a one-on-one talk. For this reason, Mom and Dad have to train their kids to be able to express themselves in front of a group of people.

HELPFUL HOW-TO HINTS

SMART STARTER   Ask Heather's teacher how well she participates in class. If she is among the top three or four kids who respond to questions and ask some themselves, all is well.

If not, start playing the "question game" with her. Ask her at least five specific questions about her classes each day, such as, "What new fact did you learn today?" Insist on answers beyond the often-heard "I don't remember."

Once you know what the new fact is, ask Heather what she thinks the teacher might talk about the next day. Then have her write down three question about what this might be.

Pretend you're the teacher and have Heather ask you the questions, which you will try to answer. Then pretend you're Heather in the middle of a class and ask some questions.

Sneak in a few silly questions during this process, so Heather will laugh and say, That's stupid, Mom. Then you explain that there are no stupid questions, except for unasked ones—and they're *really* stupid.

SUPER STARTER   With an older child, discuss the topic of grades. Most teachers count oral class participation as a certain percentage of the final grade, so there's an extra incentive to work on speaking up in class.

If Hank doesn't do well in that area, teach him to become a more active student. That means set a good example yourself, by speaking correctly and by insisting he find better words than the constant "like," "you know," and "stuff." Then help him think of comments and questions he can use in his next science class.

Help Hank expand his question-asking skills by teaching him to zoom in on the finer points of a topic. Rather than have him ask just why, have him ask, Why not? Or, What is the deeper meaning? Or, How does this connect to that?

In discussion with Hank, agree to a minimum of times he should speak up in a class, such as twice or three times, as an experiment. Then check with the teacher to see if Hank's participation grade is going up.

Notes & Quotes

_____

_____

_____

_____

_____

Don't expect a sudden change. You can't turn a quiet, passive student into a lively class extrovert overnight, but do look for improvement. Any increased speaking up in class or just even trying to participate more is an occasion to show your approval. Be proud of the process. Tell your kids, Way to go!

Remember: Praise always brings about a raise: in achievement, esteem, interest. It just works best.

The ability to become a more active student has many benefits. One of the biggest ones is the skill to know how to ask for help with a problem and to get the help you ask for.

5 | Make Yourself Heard

PARENT POINTER *Teach your kids to get attention and to solve problems.*

Are you shy yourself? Do you hate to attract attention? Do you find that sometimes in a store or office you just walk away without voicing your complaint or stating your opinion, and then you fuss and fume later at home but get nothing accomplished?

Your kids are your best imitators. They do that out of love and admiration for you. They copy your behavior and maybe even take it a step further. So make sure your kids aren't going to turn into frustrated teens who write off the world and turn to alternative measures and substances, such as violence, experimenting with drugs and alcohol, smoking, or getting involved in sex prematurely.

FYI

What better skill can you give your kids than the ability to express their opinions and make themselves heard? Or to be able to discuss any problems they might have and get help? None. This is really a life skill, not just a school skill.

During their school years, this skill brings your kids especially incredible benefits. For if they find avenues to be heard and listened to, early on, they feel secure, wanted, and honored, not only at home but also in school. This frees their minds to concentrate on the most important task at hand: learning and growing up to become healthy and productive citizens.

HELPFUL HOW-TO HINTS

SMART STARTER From the time Blake learns to speak, encourage him to express his opinions and never cut him off with a harsh comment. Don't squelch him; make him feel comfortable enough to talk with you about whatever he wants.

Teach him to be polite and respectful at the same time: to be quiet when others are talking and not be sarcastic. You do that by practicing the same rules.

Ask Blake for his opinion on something every day. Teach him to begin with "I think" or "I believe" and how to express a difference of opinion: for example, "Excuse me, but I disagree," or "Forgive me, but this is the way I see it." In short, be the conduit through which Blake can make his view of the world known.

In school he also needs a way to express what's on his mind. That starts with his teacher. Always have Blake take his concerns to the teacher first. If he has something beyond the classroom that worries him, find out the procedure for notifying the guidance counselor, principal, or resource officer and help Blake take his concern to them. In short, teach Blake how to make himself and his worries heard and then follow up on them. At times, you may have to step in and see what is being done to correct the problems.

SUPER STARTER

As kids get older, many more troubling issues arise, so they have to know where to go to complain in school, and how to complain, and to whom. Explain to Blair that to have a problem at school or to see or hear something that is wrong, or even make a mistake herself, is not the worst thing she can do; the worst thing is not to tell you or the teacher about it.

Name the dangerous things kids face these days, and they are violence, drugs, drinking, smoking, and prematurely engaging in sex. Explain to Blair the dangers of these activities, how they can harm kids and reduce their potential, even hurt them permanently, or cause others irreparable harm.

Go over the school rules or the student handbook with Blair and tell her where to turn if she sees friends breaking the rules and engaging in harmful activities.

Practice at home with Blair as to how she should report on the problems she observes. Blair doesn't want to become a tattletale, but she must be taught to let the teacher, guidance counselor, principal, or resource officer know what she has observed. Any student threatening another or bragging about a weapon or wanting to harm a teacher must be reported immediately. If Blair is able to talk to you, you can take the concern from there.

If Blair is being picked on, or if she tells you about other kids getting picked on, do not wait another moment. Go to the school and insist that something be done. There are so many solutions—kids' schedules can be changed; they can be moved to other classes—but the bullies and those being bullied must get help immediately. If not, a school tragedy might occur. With Blair's help, you can prevent that. Get going. Right now.

Notes & Quotes

_____

_____

_____

_____

_____

This takes us to the end of the first section of this book. It's time for a pause and some applause. Smile and plan a reward for your kids. Tell them, You're terrific. We're getting smarter *together*.

At this point you've finished the hardest part of making your kids smarter. You have turned your kids into better listeners, more aware students, and more caring participants and citizens. You have laid a solid groundwork, a strong foundation. It's much easier from now on, because all you have to do is build on that foundation.

Part II: Library Smarts

Help your kids to . . .
know all about the library and its resources

It is important for any learner to know where and how to learn more, how to dig into a topic of interest, how to search for facts and information. In short, how to research.

For that reason, it's vital for you to equip your kids with the keys to a place that contains everything they will ever need to know: a library. It doesn't matter whether it's a school library or a public one, a university library or a commercial one. To that category also belong all the bookstores, from small neighborhood ones to the giants you find in the mall or in freestanding buildings. They all come under the heading of repository for books.

In that repository we find the collections we want our kids to be thrilled about. Every visit to one of those places will make them a little smarter.

6 | Love the Library

PARENT POINTER *Teach your kids to love libraries and bookstores.*

Do you visit your public library often? Seldom? Never? Do you know the librarian and the library assistants? If not, do you drop into bookshops and browse around? And if not that, do you access Internet bookstores or check out the holdings of the Library of Congress? Let's admit it, whether you're a frequent visitor or not, the library (either close to your home or housed in cyberspace) is a smorgasbord of knowledge. Your kids need to know all its benefits.

FYI

Many teachers report that kids know the layouts and offerings of video stores like the backs of their hands. Their parents have taken them along from early childhood when they rent movies for the weekend. Yet libraries and bookstores offer what the video stores do plus innumerable other items.

Furthermore, libraries and bookstores are hands-on places, where actual sampling of the material is encouraged. Kids need to do that: flip through books, look at the pictures, read the chapter headings, and then find a corner and curl up with something really good to read.

HELPFUL HOW-TO HINTS

SMART STARTER Take Carla to her favorite library or bookstore once a week, or at least as often as you take her to the video store

Help her know all the kinds of materials that are available in the town library. What types of books do they have? What magazines? What newspapers? Tapes, CDs, and, yes, videos also? Let her check out a volume.

Next, branch out, take Carla to the closest university library, and let her use the computer to see if they have any works by an author she recognizes. Then take a tour with her of the library facilities. Be sure she gets to see the valuable documents, the special historical collections, and the early printed works, tomes, and folios.

Pick up a schedule of special events. What summer programs does the library have? When is a children's author coming to speak? In short, make sure that libraries and bookstores are among Carla's favorite places to visit. They will be if you let her wander around the children's section and pick out some books that thrill her. Then say, Let's hurry home so we can read the books, OK?

SUPER STARTER To get Carson charged up about libraries, begin with his interest. Remember his passion for arrowheads last year, and how he plotted Indian trails? Ask him to make a list of his favorite topics and then enlist the help of the librarian or bookstore clerk. And place some "cool" materials on order, so Carson will have something to look forward to. For his birthday, give him a bookstore gift certificate and encourage him to spend it on his favorite authors.

Find out if there's a reading circle for older kids or start one yourself: an hour a week when kids Carson's age get together and discuss kids' classics. When you give Carson his weekly allowance, split the cash in half: one half to spend as he wishes, the other for books.

Get permission for you both to visit the enormous number of stacks just crammed full with books, periodicals, journals, and encyclopedias in almost every language of the world that are housed at the nearby university campus. Make it a special field trip, just the two of you. Afterward, stop by the campus bookstore and let him browse there, mingle with the students, and buy something to read. You do the same. In short, through your actions make Carson realize how very special libraries and all other places devoted to books are.

Then, after you get back home, both of you settle down comfortably with your books, examine them, and talk. Wasn't that fun today? Then start planning your next adventure to the library or bookstore.

Notes & Quotes

_____

_____

_____

_____

On the next journey to the library, you'll want to get into the specifics. For there isn't a topic in the universe that the library or the librarian doesn't have some information on or some reference for.

The next trick is to be smart enough to find out the facts yourself and make sure your kids can do the same. To make that work, you need to know the basic library arrangements, but that isn't hard. Once you've got the basic system down, you can always look it up again. But it's great to have an overview, especially for kids.

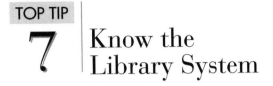

7 Know the Library System

PARENT POINTER *Teach your kids to know the arrangement of library materials.*

How are the materials in the library arranged? If you were in charge, how would you catalog them?

FYI

Most smaller libraries use the Dewey Decimal System to classify their materials. The system is named after Melvil Dewey, an American librarian who invented it in 1876. His system divides all publications into ten major categories. If kids have a general idea of these divisions, they'll save time when tracking down books about subjects that interest them.

000–099 General works: encyclopedias and reference books

100–199 Philosophy, psychology, behavior

200–299 Religion: world religions, mythology

300–399 Social science: law, government, education, economics

400–499 Philology: languages, grammar, dictionaries

500–599 Science: physics, chemistry, botany, zoology, mathematics

600–699   Other science fields: radio, engineering, aviation

700–799   Fine arts: music, painting, architecture, sports, theater

800–899   Literature: plays, poetry, essays, fiction

900–999   History, biography, geography, travel

From this table you notice that all books on religion, for example, have a number between 200 and 299.

But the Dewey Decimal System goes beyond that. It subdivides each major division into ten groups and then divides them again. To illustrate, let's look at literature (800–899).

800–899   Literature

810   American Literature

811   Poetry

812   Drama

814   Essays

820   English Literature

821   Poetry

822   Drama

And so on. The classification number is written on the spine of the book. It's referred to as a *call number*.

Reference books are shelved together and usually marked with an *R*.

Fiction books—novels and short-story collections by a single author—occupy a special section in the library and are arranged alphabetically by the author's last name.

HELPFUL HOW-TO HINTS

SMART STARTER Since you know Mike likes made-up adventure stories, all he needs to know is that they're fiction to go to that section and look for the authors' last names. If he knows the name of the author, he can easily find them himself. To widen Mike's reading horizon, give him a list of authors recommended by his teachers or the school librarian. Then watch him locate the books, look at the covers, and select one, two, or three to check out.

Also during the week, when Mike mentions something that interests him, make a note—DINOSAURS or MARCO POLO or ICE HOCKEY—then show him the Dewey Decimal chart, and ask him to tell you to which division his topic belongs.

On the next visit to the library, watch Mike become a book sleuth and track down something that interests him. Some libraries have card catalogs with index cards for subjects, authors, and titles. Most now have their catalog on computer files, using the same categories: subjects, authors, titles. Turn Mike loose, ask him to lead you to the correct aisle of books, and beam as he finds the book or books he's been looking for.

SUPER STARTER With Mandy, who is older, check to see what she knows abut the Dewey Decimal System. Ask her, Since books are shelved by number in their order of classification, what comes first, books on mathematics or books on engineering?

Next, ask Mandy to choose any of the following and tell where in her school or public library she would find books on that subject.

Rap music   Horses

American political parties   History of Cape Town

Ceramics   Cheese omelets

Better, let Mandy choose her own topics of interest and tell what call numbers belong to them. What are some titles her school library has on the topics she cares about? If there isn't much, get Mandy to choose three books she'd like to see in her school library and then ask the librarian if you may contribute one or all three of them.

Finally, ask Mandy to pick up any three books in your house and tell where they might be found in the library. Have her explain why, then ask her, Can you think of a better method to arrange all printed materials? Mention the existence of the Library of Congress system.

Notes & Quotes

_____

_____

_____

_____

_____

Also think of the Dewey Decimal System when talking about career choices with your kids; each of the main categories can lead to hundreds of special interests to explore.

There are job possibilities too numerous to count. Open your children's eyes; let them see the richness of life, the many possibilities, the vastness of human endeavor and achievement.

After that discussion, which might lead to how reading tastes have changed since 1876—even the books themselves have evolved from regular volumes to audiotapes, large-print editions, computer down-loadables, and other formats—say, Hey, I'm impressed. You know how to track down fascinating books.

But, you tell them, there are many more materials available than just books. Why limit yourself to one source of information when there are tons out there? The trick is to get your kids' curiosity up.

What else is there besides books and stuff? they'll ask. Let's find out.

8 Know the Library Materials

It's the "and stuff" you really want your kids to know about. So make investigating that the next adventure you go on.

PARENT POINTER *Teach your kids the different kinds of library materials.*

When was the last time you looked up something in an encyclopedia? An almanac or yearbook? A dictionary or an atlas? Of course, I mean the actual books, not just on the screen while doing a computer search. It's been a while, right?

And what about all those other reference materials, such as the pamphlets in the vertical file, or the microfilm and microfiche collections? What about special dictionaries, such as *Webster's Biographical Dictionary*, the *Statistical Abstract of the United States, Current Biography, Who's Who*, Bartlett's *Familiar Quotations,* and the *Short Story Index*? Just think of all the millions of things that have come out in print, since Johannes Gutenberg invented printing from movable type over five hundred years ago, and of all the books of lists, explanations, and summaries. How in the world are they all stored, indexed, cross-referenced?

A bibliographer can tell you.

FYI

A bibliographer is someone who knows about the cataloging, description, and sources of printed matter, old and new. The word comes from *biblio* (Greek for book) and *graph* (to write). They're actually sleuths who can track down tracts, be they by Martin Luther or Lao-tzu, in no time. Along with reference librarians, bibliographers are a library's detectives. Some of their enormous research skill is what you want to give your kids, so they'll have all kinds of materials and methods of research at their fingertips, now and for the rest of their lives.

HELPFUL HOW-TO HINTS

SMART STARTER Begin by asking Jamila what her favorite birds are. If she says "big ones," help her narrow "big birds" down, for example, to puffins. Then have her look up *puffins* in an encyclopedia and learn that they are seabirds living in northern regions.

Next, have her draw a puffin and maybe an outline of Alaska, using a child's atlas as a guide. That might lead to her researching how maps of Alaska used to look, which requires locating an older atlas in a nearby university library. Show her the changes in maps over the years.

Also, while talking to the reference librarian, ask to see the earliest pictures of seabirds that they have. Then ask Jamila how many puffins exist today, and help her look up the answer in a reference book.

Post all her research information on a bulletin board in her room, so she can be proud of what she found out and have a record of how she went about it.

SUPER STARTER Meanwhile Jamal, several years older, wants to find out about the first baseball game ever played. He'll consult an almanac on the date. Then he'll find out the name of the biggest newspaper in New York City and check if baseball existed in 1899. Turns out this game started much earlier, in 1823, when it was called base ball. Next might come checking out a reel of microfilm, loading the reader, and manipulating it until the first newspaper article (in *The National Advocate*) appears on the screen.

Closer to home, take Jamal on a tour to his hometown paper to see how far back their archives go and what their sports section reported on the game, if the paper existed back then.

Next is a search for the program of the first baseball game ever played in Jamal's hometown. If it's available, it's probably kept in the vertical file of Jamal's city library. You and he can go there and check.

While there, please introduce Jamal to the *Readers' Guide to Periodical Literature*, which will list the major articles and stories written on his favorite baseball team. Investigating all those articles will keep him busy for a while. He may even start taking a few notes.

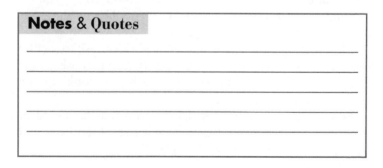

Notes & Quotes

That's great, just great. You can't praise your kids enough for getting interested. And that leads you directly to another huge skill they need to make them smarter.

Kids who are turning into information sleuths are on a roll. They're intent on finding out more and more about a subject.

As your children's interest expands, so does their quest for yet more knowledge. For that reason, turn your kids lose to investigate more, but not before teaching them the next important skill.

9 | Avoid Plagiarism

PARENT POINTER *Teach your kids what plagiarism is and how to avoid it.*

Do you tap into cable TV without paying for it? Fill up your car with gasoline and then drive off without settling your bill? Of course not, though at times the thought might occur to you, as it does to everybody. Wouldn't it be great to find a million dollars and walk off with it?

The reality is, it's fun to wonder once in a while about getting away with taking something that's not yours. But of course we can't and won't do that. We can't and won't steal. That also goes for the treasures found in books.

FYI

We may pick up facts and information at will and talk about them freely. Yet when it comes to taking notes, we need to quote from the source, give credit to the author, and cite the book or journal that provided the information to us.

Otherwise we're committing *plagiarism*, which means we're stealing words and ideas from a writer, reporter, or poet. This has become a real problem in recent years because the computer makes it so easy to download whatever information we're looking for. Luckily your kids won't ever have to worry about being accused of plagiarism, because you're teaching them to avoid it.

HELPFUL HOW-TO HINTS

SMART STARTER Just as you taught Ricky that we don't take something that's not ours, in the same way, he needs to know he can't copy a page from a book and hand it in as his own report. What you do is encourage Ricky to *paraphrase*, restate in his own words, what he reads. Say, Can you say that in your own words?

From then on, have him read a paragraph and write down what he read, always using his own words.

Next, show him how to enclose a phrase or sentence in quotation marks, if he wants to use the author's exact words, and how to give the author credit.

SUPER STARTER With Rene, who is in fifth grade, examine a textbook with footnotes or endnotes and explain what they are: indications of the source of the information in the main text. In other words, this is where the author got certain facts or examples.

When Rene does her next science report, help her restate the information she's gathered, using her own vocabulary. Say, What do these sentences mean? Help her change all the words, then shorten and combine sentences.

If Rene insists on including an important point in the author's own words, show her how to give proper credit. These days it may be enough to put a number in parentheses, after the copied sentence in quotation marks, and add a list of sources, or bibliography, at the end of the report. If that's not enough, her teachers will tell her.

The bibliography needs the author's name (last name first), the title of the book (underlined or in italics), plus the name of the publisher, place, and date.

For example:
Edwards, Rene. *The Day of the Puffin.* Northboro, Alaska: Smarter Students Press, 2002.

Notes & Quotes

_____

_____

_____

_____

_____

There are several different ways to go about giving credit to a source, but the main thing is to teach your kids from the start that they should compliment the authors whose words they're quoting. They do that by listing the authors' works, so that teachers and others reading their reports can go back and look for more information if they want to.

The last school tool involving libraries is the most fun, because kids use their hands and minds when they tackle it. All they have to do is find a little extra room.

10 Set Up Your Your Own Library

PARENT POINTER *Teach your kids to start their own library and add to it periodically.*

How many bookcases are in your house? And how are the books in them arranged? Are they stacked by size, from tallest to shortest book, or vice versa? Or by whatever way you can cram them in? Or in some other kind of system?

FYI

Reading is *everything* in education, because that's the best way to gain knowledge. So congratulations if you have a house filled with books and magazines. They should be everywhere—on end tables, by the bed, on counters, and in your car's glove compartment. They should beam from bookcases, for the more books that are in your house, the more reading is a part of your family and the smarter your kids will be.

It's time to go shopping.

HELPFUL HOW-TO HINTS

SMART STARTER First check Megan's room to see how much space can be squeezed out for a big bookcase of her own. Then discuss what type she'd like and go and buy one. Or have Dad build one. Or maybe the family can make one together. But this is an important project, so it needs to be discussed at length.

Once the new bookcase is in place, have Megan arrange all her books on it according to Dewey's method or, better, Megan's own method. Buy her some bookplates or have her design them herself and glue them into her books.

Ask her to make a list of all her books and start a chart on which she can check some of them out to her friends. While she's doing that, she can also make a list of more titles she needs.

Let her give you a "tour" of her library, and discuss with her its strong points and weak points. Does she have her own dictionary? An atlas? A basic reference book? Does she have all those children's books you love, like *Little Women*, *Peter Pan*, *A Wrinkle in Time*, *Tales from Shakespeare*, *The Wind in the Willows*, *The Black Stallion*, *The Secret Garden*, the Harry Potter books, *Charlotte's Web*, *Heidi*, *Bambi*, *Black Beauty*, *Grimm's Fairy Tales*, *Pippi Longstocking*, Bible stories . . . ? The list goes on. Just think back to your childhood and ask yourself, What were my favorites back then? Then add the latest, best selections from reading lists provided by Megan's teacher and her school librarian.

Offer Megan the choice of a children's magazine. Again, her school librarian will have the latest options, and it's going to be fun for Megan to pick one she likes.

On the bottom shelf of the new bookcase, start Megan's own vertical file. In a shoe box she can keep articles or puzzles that interest her, magazine pictures she has cut out, or her own drawings—like a real library.

SUPER STARTER   Knowing Mark, your older son, he will have watched Megan organize her library and be ready to tell you just what he needs to get *his* book collection squared away. So get him that floor-to-ceiling bookcase he's been clamoring for. Make sure it's set up securely.

One shelf can be devoted to Mark's current research interests, all the books he's reading at the moment or plans to read, and the new magazine subscription—geared to his age and interest—that you subscribe to just for him. The rest of the shelves are for his other books, plus whatever school papers he wants to keep.

And the empty shelves? They are for the big gaps his book collection has. What's missing? You and he need to find out. Mark's teacher will be only too glad to give him a list of recommended books for his grade level and beyond. Why not buy a few of those and start Mark on the road to reading ahead? Then, when those books come up during his school term, he will have been through them once already and can contribute in class and get the great grades he deserves.

Last, Mark needs to post a book wish list for when relatives call and want to know what he wants for his birthday or other special occasions. Mark's list should be constantly updated, so there will always several books listed. That gives him lots to look forward to.

Off with the TV from now on, off with the boom box and all that other noise. The computer games can wait too. You're in this together, all the members of your family. So sit down most evenings and get out something to read. Or have Megan and Mark talk about what book each of them would grab if the house were on fire or what three books they would take with them to Survivor Island. Why? Tell them what your choice would be, something you can read and reread, right? Good job.

Notes & Quotes

_____

_____

_____

_____

_____

Now your kids know what's out there—a vast universe of information. How can they master it without its mastering them? What tools can they use to pick and choose from such enormous possibilities?

How can they be in charge without getting overwhelmed by so much that's just waiting to be learned?

For that to happen, they need the best help possible. That's you, of course, plus mankind's most ingenious assistant—technology.

Part III: Computer Smarts

Help your kids to . . .

know how to use a computer

In the past thirty years we've taken a gigantic leap forward from the times when learning and studying could be very tedious. Now it's not. Now it's hot: sizzling.

The reason for this is, of course, computers. You can now give your kids untold shortcuts, speed up their learning process, and make it enjoyable. All you have to do is give them the basics of computer knowledge.

The next most important skill for any school-age kid is to know how to simplify all those mountains of school paper-work. Cut to the chase by using whatever time is available wisely, with the help of the best learning tools around. You'll be able to avoid lots of busywork and wasted hours with the help of a computer.

How wonderful it is to be able to introduce your child to cyberspace. Aren't you lucky to be raising kids in the third millennium?

11 | Know Basic Computer Skills

PARENT POINTER *Teach your kids some basic computer skills.*

How often do you use the computer at home? Every day or rarely? Do you even have one? If not, are you on the verge of getting one?

I bet you are, but whatever your answer, you know the Internet is a powerful instrument and has a tremendous influence on the lives of our kids. It is now what TV used to be in the fifties and sixties. But computer technology is much more educational than TV, since it's a two-way medium, allowing the user to interact as was never possible before.

You can now watch your kids communicate quickly with other boys and girls their age in Austria or Australia or both places (and more) at once. The Internet is a must-have home tool for school. It's basic to making our kids smarter.

FYI

What's especially great about accessing the Internet is that it's an activity for moms and dads and their kids to do *together*. The basic skill is so simple—just point and click (point your mouse arrow to a picture or word, watch it change into a mini hand with an index finger sticking up, and then press). That's all. Chances are your kids are already better at this than you. Be sure to help your kids get really comfortable with this superb tool. You want to make them and yourself at home on the Internet.

What is the Internet? Simply stated, the Internet is a huge library with all kinds of information that the computer brings to you from all over the world with the click of a mouse. It makes use of a wire-and-cable network that carries computer messages all over the universe just like a telephone.

But it does so much more. It can bring pictures, music, videos, and games directly to your desk. It's a treasure chest of world knowledge and information directly at your fingertips. I'm sure you know all that already. But do you know how it started?

Over thirty years ago, a U.S. Defense Department employee came up with a project to connect the various branches of the military and send information to different locations around the world. From that early plan, the idea grew into a commercial venture, and now it includes most businesses, schools, and organizations, offering access to innumerable places—and their information.

Like any collection of information, it has some facts and pictures you will not want your kids to see. And it is used by some groups and companies that don't have the welfare of your kids in mind at all.

So, how can you be sure your kids log on only to the positive powers of the Internet, while disregarding the negative?

Simple. You set up the computer in the family room, so you can supervise its use.

HELPFUL HOW-TO HINTS

SMART STARTER Begin by talking to Taylor to find out what he already knows about the Internet. These days, from kindergarten on, kids are exposed to Internet games and taught the ABC's of cyberspace. But you can't be sure exactly what Taylor knows and what he doesn't unless you question him.

Ask Taylor to demonstrate what he knows about the Internet. He will demonstrate his ability to play a game or two, but you will forge ahead and ask him, for example, What does the www stand for? He may know: World Wide Web.

Say to him, Is it the same as the Internet? The answer is no, the World Wide Web is part of the Internet, but not all Internet servers are part of the World Wide Web. It's estimated that there are 100 million Internet users all over the world, and many of them are from the younger generation.

Let Taylor prove to you what he really knows. Say, Show me more of what you can do on the computer; then fill in what he doesn't know. Quiz him about the following terms:

> Domain name: The registered name of the company or person the Web site is about.
>
> Index page: The starting page of the Web site.
>
> Menu: The choices in a computer program or Web site.
>
> Icons: The small pictures representing some function on a Web site.

SUPER STARTER With Tyra, who is older, you will watch over her shoulder as she navigates on the Internet.

Does she already have "Favorites" or "Favorite Places"? If not, help her with that shortcut. When she goes to a Web site for help with her homework, it will ask her if she wants to add the site to her favorites. Help her click on *yes*; then she'll always have that site handy.

Next, ask Tyra what the following stand for:

.com   (business)

.gov   (government)

.org   (organization)

.mil   (military)

.edu   (educational place)

.net   (network)

Knowing these addresses will help her decide whether the information obtained from these sites is reliable or not. Information from a commercial site is quite different from that on a university site.

Then say, Tyra, what do all those slashes in Web addresses stand for? Can you tell me? She will tell you that the words after the slash will direct you to a certain page of the Web site. Just compare the after-the-slash words to a section in a department store or an extension number on the telephone. After you reach city hall, you still need to know which floor or office you want, the mayor or the dog catcher. Same with Web site addresses.

Teach Tyra never to access information or pictures that are harmful to her. For that lesson to sink in, take her to the corner mini market and point out the shelves where lurid magazines are displayed. Say, Just like that shelf, lots of trashy stuff is on the Internet, but it's not as clearly marked as in this store. You understand? Never ever access a site that is unknown to you. And don't ever enter a chat room I haven't OK'd first. When in doubt, please ask me.

Except for that serious warning, which you will print on a sheet of paper and post above the computer, the Internet is a miracle, with which you can access the whole universe from your den. While you're posting that warning, it's best to make up a family policy on computer use as well and post it under the warning. These days many kids enjoy the computer more than the telephone. They start getting involved in "instant messaging" and, from then on, keep it up for hours. What their friend said to another friend, what she wore when she said it, what he looked like at that moment, and what was announced over the school intercom while they were walking away—all of that is of vital importance to them. So set a time limit: one hour a day computer time and thirty minutes max instant messaging during the week; violations: no computer for a week, except for homework.

Like anything else, the use of the computer has to be regulated at your house. Kids love regulations and rules. They crave structure. Therefore, give them the security of a framework. Post a schedule and congratulate your kids for sticking to it. After all, isn't it wonderful that they live in an age where they have all the best information in the world day and night at their fingertips? The Internet, employed as a savvy school tool, will make them smarter, no doubt about it.

Notes & Quotes

_____

_____

_____

_____

_____

Good for you, for encouraging your kids in correct computer use, plus keeping them safe from cyber sleaze. That's step number one. Step number two is to expand your kids' use of computers and have them go beyond the computer fun and games.

12 Learn More Advanced Computer Skills

PARENT POINTER *Teach your kids more advanced computer skills.*

Do you use your computer for researching a topic? Looking up a medical site to get advice on sore throats? Comparing dealer prices of a Camry you want to buy? Checking out real estate or stock prices? Sending Aunt Flora a bouquet of carnations for her birthday?

Kids need these skills too, but primarily for writing reports and doing more complicated homework. Help them by investigating how much they know already. Have they taken a class on computer skills in school? When did they learn keyboarding, or didn't they?

FYI

No matter what they know, it's best to review what you know with them. Ask them about the following terms:

> link and hyperlink: they connect you to other parts of the Web site or to other sites
>
> scroll: find the up or down arrows on the right-hand side of the screen, then point and click to see if there is more information you like

back button: the button on the top of the screen that moves you back to a previous Web page

downloading: copying a program from the Internet onto your computer's hard drive and saving it

various search engines and directories: Web site sections that search the whole Web to locate numerous Web sites on your topic, such as

http://www.yahoo.com

http://www.google.com

http://search.aol.com

http://www.go.com

http://www.excite.com

Of course, you want to use these directories and search engines first, to find the best Web sites made just for kids.

Furthermore, you want your kids to be able to use word-processing skills to really make use of what information they can scout out.

HELPFUL HOW-TO HINTS

SMART STARTER Introduce Ryan to www.dictionary.com, which contains not only definitions of words but also word-search games and words similar to the one she's already used three times in her report.

Next let her browse the Bronx Zoo with the help of http://www.bronxzoo.com and click on the Kids Only link. There she can read up on all kinds of animal facts and then decide what to include in the homework assignment she has for school.

Ryan can then expand her knowledge on zebras by advancing to http://www.worldalmanacforkids.com, which is World Almanac for Kids.

Finally, have Ryan type her report, using the word-processing components of the computer, and have her use the spell checker to help with the proofreading.

SUPER STARTER Randy, who is older, will already know where to find the information he needs on the Internet, but he will still come to you for help with his report. So ask him to type his rough draft.

Next, teach him to read it out loud, which may help him see that his information is all jumbled up. Show him how to delete sentences, how to rearrange and move paragraphs, and how to copy and paste text. Last, show Randy how to use the HELP section of the word processor.

In the end, Randy will print out a final copy, and the next day he'll be first in class to hand in his report. He may want to tutor a less capable student in doing the same. Some kids learn best when they are the teacher. Take them all out for pizza the following weekend. Have fun, and Randy and his friends will remember it for a long time.

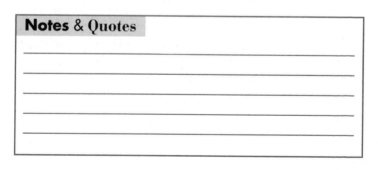

Notes & Quotes

In the old days, reports would have taken many hours of moans and groans and countless erasures. Now it's a fast assignment.

The basic keyboarding skills used in writing reports can be put to an even better use: e-mail.

TOP TIP

13 Use E-Mail

PARENT POINTER *Help your kids send and receive e-mail.*

Do you stay in touch with your family via e-mail? Do you send your vacation pictures to your sister? A photo of your new puppy to your parents? Memos from work to your colleagues?

FYI

While e-mail hasn't replaced snail mail, it has definitely enticed more people into corresponding. It's fabulous to send a message to someone and know it'll get there in a matter of seconds or minutes. Even telegrams take longer, let alone regular postal delivery. And to know you can send an e-letter to several friends and have it waiting for them when they log on, that's amazing. Plus, it's time saving, cost effective, and easy. Imagine having to run to the post office and get out a dozen envelopes that you've hand addressed. Think of getting dressed, hopping into the car, driving to the mailing place— all that time and postage plus the hassle of standing in line. But none of that comes into play when you have the addresses already stored in your e-address book. You just type the letter. Then it's only a matter of point, click—and quick!—the recipients are reading your words while, still in your pj's, you sip your latte and stretch luxuriously. You can stay in touch with the whole universe.

That's what you want your kids to learn.

HELPFUL HOW-TO HINTS

SMART STARTER Teach Lindsay how to send an e-mail message to her cousin. Tell her to type slowly and read the message aloud to herself before she sends it. It's best to have her avoid any mistakes. While e-mail is more informal than traditional mail, everything Lindsay sends out should be written as correctly as possible.

While waiting for a reply, instruct Lindsay never to open an e-mail not meant for her, and not to open e-mail addressed to her from senders whose names or addresses she does not know. She wouldn't get letters from your neighbor's mailbox and open them, would she? She probably doesn't receive snail mail from strangers, but you'd want her to let you open it if she did. So, if she isn't the intended recipient or doesn't recognize the name or address of the sender, she needs to be taught not to open e-mail either. Mail from strangers is probably just an advertisement, but it might contain a virus that would attack the computer. Or it could be cyber trash, and you don't want Lindsay exposed to trash.

Next, show her how to e-mail a grandparent, teacher, or coach. Before she starts, have her formulate a question she wants to ask. It's best to stick to one or two questions when e-mailing, so the letter won't be too long.

After that, show Lindsay how to delete her e-mail messages unless they're special. In that case, she may want to print them out and make a booklet out of them ("Points to Ponder from Papa"?).

Finally, find out what excites Lindsay. Is it basketball, Barbies, ballet? Whatever the topic, show Lindsay how she can e-mail for more information. There is always a society, museum, or business that has the latest information plus background facts on Lindsay's hobby, anything from a camp or lesson to an exhibit dealing with what she's interested in. And now is a good time for her to learn to send e-thank-you notes, maybe some with special borders. Polite e-correspondence is best learned early.

SUPER STARTER Liam, who is older, already has his e-mail pals; please, teach him never to be rude. Cruel and hurtful statements, once e-mailed, can never be taken back. Most likely a "friend" will forward them to another "friend," and then trouble can start. Curse words also are no-no's, so no cussing. It's best to post a reminder near the computer.

Next, help Liam find e–pen pals among kids his age in another country. His teachers or librarian can help you there. Exchanging information with a student from overseas will teach Liam more than just what's in the notes he gets. It'll empower him to know he has made a connection to someone his age in another part of the e-world.

Now, when Liam is enraged about the unfairness of things, let him use e-mail to express his opinion, but in a mature and polite way. He can compose a letter to the editor of the newspaper, revise it, save it as draft, print it out to see what it looks like, and finally send it when it best says what he wants it to say. What a thrill it will be for him if his letter to the editor is printed the following week!

That thrill will even heighten when Liam starts getting tons of real mail. That will happen when he requests pamphlets on whatever products and programs interest him. He can also start e-mailing for information on his favorite college team, or his favorite college. It's never too early to investigate his dreams.

Finally, e-mailing is best when it's done by you. Every day, or several times a week, send your kids a short e-mail or a special reminder about what you want them to do. Then include a question that'll require them to e-mail back. Remember, e-mail can cut through a lot of misunderstandings. It can simplify things. Kids often respond to a written message better than to an oral one. They do their chores better when they are posted; how can they argue with a computer screen? That way, always keep the lines of communication open between you and Lindsay and Liam. If you were wrong in an argument, type I'M SORRY.

Also, if you're a mom or dad who shares custody or sees your kids only once a week, what a great way to begin a daily on-line lifeline. That means you're e-mailing Liam every day and asking him about his classes, prodding him to learn more, suggesting to him more things to read and study. You become his study buddy and laugh together when he knows more than you do and vice versa. You may not be able to see him every day, but your words will await him. E-parenting is the next best thing to 24/7 parenting.

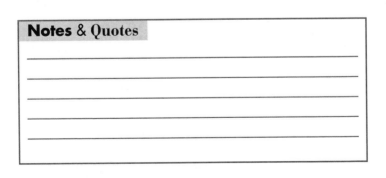

Notes & Quotes

Remember, e-mails can bring messages from the heart quickly and sincerely. So during your lunch break or even before going to work, sit down and tap out a little note of guidance or encouragement to those you treasure most. Just tell them how much you love them and how proud you are of them. And what a wonderful life lies ahead.

Another great advantage of the computer is its use as a planner, a scheduler. It should be your home secretary. Better yet, make it your kids' secretary, so their lives can be easier.

14 | Get Organized with the Help of a Computer

PARENT POINTER *Help your kids get organized with a computer.*

Are you using the Internet for bill paying? Checking up on your stocks? Planning your finances for the future? Then you're in a great position to help your kids further their computer skills. But even if you're not, you can get them started on getting organized.

FYI

Organization, or the lack of it, can make or break your kids on their way to being the best students they can be. These days, with everybody's schedule so crazy, you know yourself that if you don't write down key dates and appointments you're likely to start floundering halfway through the week.

Kids have even less ability to get themselves squared away when it comes to deadlines, major projects, and big exams, so show them how to use their personal computer as a faithful secretary.

Helpful How-To Hints

SMART STARTER Before schools starts, sit down with Abdul at the computer and help him decide on a personal school calendar. He can use a special software program or design his own. Then have him fill in his yearly schedule, using the school calendar he'll bring home. Excitedly, he'll type in dates for upcoming vacations and holidays, plus teachers' workdays and conference days. In a short while, he'll have his whole school year mapped out.

Next, as soon as school starts and his teacher explains her weekly schedule, have Abdul list his weekly tests and assignments, at least for the first grading period. Then comes the creative part in planning—setting up mini deadlines. If his spelling test is every Friday, then on Wednesdays he fills in: START STUDYING THE WEEKLY SPELLING WORDS, or LEARN HALF OF LIST. On Thursday, of course, his assignment will be: FINISH STUDYING WORDS, or LEARN SECOND HALF OF LIST. The same procedure should be followed for all announced deadlines or assignments. For example, if his teacher expects him to read twenty minutes every evening, Abdul can go ahead and fill that in for the whole semester.

Abdul will keep adding other school-related requirements to his calendar, such as meetings of the Safety Patrol Club he belongs to and all his after-school activities. Finally, you and Abdul look over his calendar together. He'll proudly print out a copy for the first week, which he'll post in his room or on the fridge or, even better, in both places.

SUPER STARTER As for Aretha, who is older, all you have to do is show her your own plan book as an example and then turn her loose on the computer. In no time she'll have designed a calendar of her own, with all the basics filled in.

Next comes setting the pre-deadlines. Tell Aretha to estimate how much time that big history project might take and fill in earlier mini deadlines on her calendar. Encourage her by saying that this year will be her best ever. Then have her plan her homework and study schedule for the first month. The second month may require a change, depending on her test results. Also have her fill in her extra-reading schedule or her independent advanced study work, plus all the outside activities that she participates in.

Then take a good hard look. You don't want to overburden her. Maybe this is the year to cut back. Most kids shouldn't have more than one or two extracurriculars. In the area of after-school activities, less is best. Please see that Aretha has plenty of time for fun things and some free time with nothing scheduled, so she can relax and enjoy life. It's very important to include blocks of time with nothing major to do.

You and Aretha should review her schedule often and change it. Also split up the supervision of her academic growth. Mom takes over the subjects that she's best in, Dad takes his favorites to help plan and encourage Aretha. Or involve a grandparent or older sibling, so Aretha has several home tutors.

If there are no school-assigned major projects, check to see what's going on. You might let Aretha come up with some of her own and work toward them. Throughout the year, keep a record of her grades and insist on steady progress and a rise in scores. Often, a time shift toward spending more minutes on her weaker subjects is called for.

Let Aretha plan the other aspects of her life with the help of the computer. Maybe allowance budgeting will be next on her list, maybe a plan for saving for a big splurge she has in mind. Also encourage her to divvy up her weekly household chores. Mom or Dad can also explain how much they'd pay an outsider to come in and clean out the garage, and Aretha and Abdul can underbid this amount and snag that extra cash.

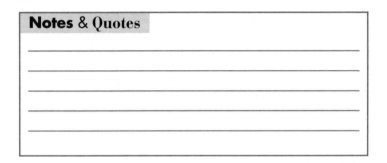

Notes & Quotes

Beyond a computer's ability to help your kids get better organized, there are numerous other great uses. For instance, the next one: journaling.

15 | Keep a Computer Log

PARENT POINTER *Help your kids keep a computer journal.*

Do you keep a journal, diary, or log on the computer? Maybe you just jot down the most important events that occur in your family, so you can write that long holiday letter in the fall and not leave out much of what happened to your family. However you use the computer, this is an easy way to record big and small events in your life, isn't it?

FYI

Many people now record their daily events in the form of e-diaries and e-journals. For some it's a wish to share what they love, others use this activity to lessen stress, and still others see it as a way to show the world they matter. Of course, what matters most to you is your kids.

HELPFUL HOW-TO HINTS

SMART STARTER For that reason, have Candee start her own off-line journal, using the word processor. She won't have to worry about spelling or sentence construction here. Just ask her to write something every day and express her feelings on anything she likes. This activity will soon become a favorite outlet. Even if she'll do it only once in a while, it will help her relax. It's fun to type along on the keyboard, giggling when words pop up on the screen with silly spelling errors or every sentence ends with a :-) or a :-(.

Next start a family journal with Candee, writing alternate entries. One day it's her turn; the next day, it's yours. Also, whenever Candee gets back a graded paragraph or written report from her teacher, have her type that report or paragraph over in a file called Candee's Keepers.

On a rainy day when she has nothing else to do, ask Candee to write a journal entry from the point of view of a raindrop. Or of her favorite teddy, Mr. Snooze.

Soon she might start writing a book about her stuffed animals and record their life stories, "as told to Candee."

SUPER STARTER Cory, who is older and into basketball, will want to keep a computer log of famous athletes and their stats. He'll chart the Charlotte Hornets' progress, for instance, and add his own stats, if he's already playing on a team. If he's interested in family history, he can trace the family name, with your help, and do a family newsletter on what he finds. Learning more about his heritage can be fascinating.

Of course, he can keep a regular journal on the computer as well, plus a "future" journal in which he'll post his ideas and dreams about what'll happen to him in high school and college. On your next day off, take him to a nearby university campus so he can watch college students using their computers during lectures. Watching them not only take notes but do fancy charts and graphs as well will inspire him. And you and Cory can explore even more software and benefit from working and wondering together.

Notes & Quotes

_____

_____

_____

_____

_____

Good for you, Mom or Dad, for teaching your children to avail themselves of the immense pluses of computer technology while avoiding the minuses. You have an incredible helper in the house to make your kids smarter—under your supervision, of course.

Next comes a huge skill that will truly change your kids' lives. It can catapult them from the ranks of kids just passing a subject to those on the honor roll.

Part IV: Study Smarts

Help your kids to . . .
learn how to really study

Now that your kids have some basic background, plus a knowledge of where information can be found and how it can be accessed and mastered, they need to prove they *have* that knowledge. It isn't enough to take in new learning. If it can't be shown to have been absorbed, much is lost. If students can't display their knowledge, their quiz scores will always be low.

Let's state the problem: How should kids study so they get the top grades they deserve? To get great test scores, kids have to have some study smarts. Let's help them snag those next.

Top study smarts begin with a love affair. The next most important school skill for learners is to fall in love with books, for it's books that hold the key to their future success. What an enormous gift you will give your kids now—the love of books.

16 Learn to Love Books

PARENT POINTER *Teach your kids to love books.*

Do you have a favorite book, one you keep reading over and over? What is it? If you have more than one, what are they?

FYI

Most people have at least one beloved book, although they may not have had a chance to look at it in years. They're too caught up in their daily lives to climb into the attic and dig out that dog-eared old *Winnie-the-Pooh.* Yet they easily agree with Emily Dickinson, who wrote:

> *There is no frigate like a book*
> *To take us lands away,*
> *Nor any coursers like a page*
> *Of prancing poetry.*

For besides just loving a book for its suspenseful story or heartfelt message, we all realize what books do. Each one, in its own way, is a vehicle to transport us into a new territory of learning.

HELPFUL HOW-TO HINTS

SMART STARTER Sit down with Alvis and explain to him to the awesomeness of a book. Books originated as a way to keep oral traditions from being lost. In ancient times, when there were too many prayers, rituals, sagas, and records to remember, people attempted to write them down. And that rough collection of various things eventually became the first book.

Pick up any book and show Alvis how far books have come from that first handmade attempt. Now we have billions of beautiful books, with glossy jackets, easy-to-read pages, intriguing chapter headings, amazing illustrations, and indexes. Ask Alvis if he'd like to write a book someday. Tell him if you would and what *your* book might be about. At this point also mention your best-loved books, and how your tastes have changed over the years. Then ask him, What's your favorite book so far?

If Alvis can name a book, build on that knowledge. Help him make a list of other titles by that author, or find authors who write on similar topics, or just take him to the bookstore and let him search for new books. Then every week, when it's time to buy groceries, swing by the library or bookstore and get Alvis another of his favorites.

Make it a real adventure, a book treasure hunt, to find good reading material for him while you scout out something good for yourself. You can get lots of help from Alvis's schoolbooks, which often include suggested reading lists, or get supplementary lists from his teacher, the town librarian, the bookstore, or the Internet.

Then have the best talks ever with Alvis about what he's reading. Tell him what chapter you're on. Make it a friendly competition as to who finishes a book first.

SUPER STARTER   In the case of Avian, who is older, let her join a book club specializing in books for her age. Her teacher or school librarian will guide you. Also ask her to interview relatives and adults in the neighborhood and find out what their favorite books were when they were her age, so she can try them. Some of them will be classics. What a great experience that will be. Avian can also write weekly book reports for the youth section of the church bulletin or synagogue newsletter. "This week Avian recommends . . ."

Next tell Avian that many children around the world would love to have her used books. Can she start a book collection at school and send the donations overseas, maybe to an orphanage in Ukraine? Are there developing nations whose school libraries are short of funds and would welcome Avian's collection with open arms? Why not let her find out?

You and Avian together can start a PTA-recommended reading list for every grade level, with recommendations from Avian and her friends. That could lead to a twice-a-year book exchange at school, where all the kids bring in books and swap them. Avian and her friends can plan the details—with your help, of course.

Finally, again with your help, Avian can e-mail schools around the world and find out what kids on other continents love to read. Most schools in foreign countries teach English, often from fourth grade on. So Avian can link up school after school in a favorite-book bond that will entice kids everywhere to read more. Just think—you're starting this ripple effect.

Notes & Quotes

_____

_____

_____

Yes, now you're really motivating your children to become better students, for the more they read, the more they know. And the more they know, the more they grow inside. What a joy it is for you to see them so excited about reading.

While you're busy getting your kids into books, you're also increasing their rate of retention. Soon they'll remember more of what they read. How can you make sure of that? Easy.

Remember Emily Dickinson's comparison of a book to a ship on a voyage to new lands? But to best benefit from such a voyage, shouldn't the traveler pack a camera or a videocam, so exciting new sights won't soon be forgotten? Of course.

In the same manner, your kids need tools to help them remember the new terrain in their minds. In other words, new facts and figures. Especially in school, it isn't just enough to take in new information; it's also important to be able to recall it later, when it's needed.

17 Take Good Notes

PARENT POINTER *Teach your kids to take good notes.*

You take notes every week when you make a grocery list, or jot down facts at a meeting, or when you fill in your to-do lists. So you know how to put things down on paper. You've used that skill for years. And at times you've felt like knocking yourself in the head because you didn't write everything down that you should have, right?

FYI

Right. So don't let your kids make the same mistake. They need this skill today far more than you do. Most school days include whole blocks of time when note-taking is required. From this moment on, teach your kids to take them properly.

Top students take top notes. Those barely squeaking by in school are the ones who lack this important skill. Your kids are going to be top students, make no mistake about it.

HELPFUL HOW-TO HINTS

SMART STARTER Ask Mya to let you look at one of her notebooks. Read over her notes. If they're clear and fairly neat, OK. But if the pages are mostly blank, tell her not to worry. You'll teach her a new system, starting now.

Begin by reading a paragraph in a book or newspaper together, and ask her what the main idea is. Discuss it, agree on what it is, and write it down on paper. Do another paragraph and another, until Mya gets the idea.

Explain that her teacher's lecture (talking) is like hearing a paragraph. The student's job is to pick out the main idea from what the teacher says. That may be: What happened, when, where, why, and who did it? Then read a paragraph aloud to Mya, and watch her write down the main idea. Have her read one to you, and you write down the key facts.

Then talk about something that interests you. Stop after a minute and ask Mya to tell you what your key ideas were. Go on to a TV program, or play a tape or a radio program. Each time have her find the main points.

Buy Mya a highlighter in her favorite color, pink. Turn her loose with new reading material, a child's magazine, and ask her to underline the key ideas. Now she has step one under control.

Step two is to just memorize the key points. That's done by teaching her to study her notes productively. Test her, using her underlined facts: How quickly can she remember the important points?

For fun, set a kitchen timer and see who can remember more facts in thirty seconds. She may surprise you and recall ten while you only remember eight. No matter, Mya's on the right track now. She will be sure to gather the correct information in class and then buckle down and learn it.

SUPER STARTER

Maris, who is older, may say his teacher doesn't give any notes. "He just tells us stories about the presidents and stuff." Which ones? you'll ask. "Oh, you know, George Washington." Great, you say, here. Give him a sheet of paper and say, Write down everything you know about our first president. Then check the paper. If it's almost blank, say, That's OK. Then explain how important note-taking is and help Maris find the relevant key points in his history-book chapter and jot them down in his notebook.

Using a stopwatch, see how many facts you and Maris can cram in in a short time period. "No fair," Maris will complain. "You already know all this stuff. You learned it in school." That's right, and now you're going to learn too, you say, smiling.

Begin with the subject that Maris likes best and show him how to study it more efficiently. Teach him how to check his recall by listing everything he knows about a topic on another blank sheet. His notes (in the notebook) and what he puts on the blank sheet with his notebook or textbook closed should look similar.

Next, have Maris record on his tape recorder what he knows about the Civil War *before* he studies it. Repeat the process *after* he has studied. Keep checking his classroom notes every day, and have him add a half page of notes from the textbook every time he comes home from school with nothing written down. That's excellent practice. Also, once Maris starts taking better notes, ask him to rewrite them on days when he has less homework than usual. The more he goes over the information taught in class, the better he'll remember it.

Ask Maris to have a study session with his friends, that you'll supervise, before a major test. Look over the notebooks of all of Maris's friends during that time. If you have saved any old college notebooks, now is a good time to bring them out and have the kids criticize them.

Start a contest, "Best Notes of the Week." Check Maris's history notebook every day, and together you and he pick the one day's notes that are most impressive. Then show him how to go over those notes, underline key points, and write them on note cards. Keep the note cards close at hand and play a game with Maris before the test—the Prediction game. You predict how many points he'll know, and he predicts how many he'll know. Then find out who is right, laugh, and get back to more schoolwork.

Notes & Quotes

_____

_____

_____

_____

_____

Don't be shocked if your children's notebooks become the best in the class. But even if they don't, you can count on their note-taking skills improving drastically. And while you're busy working on upgrading that skill, please praise your kids freely. Praise them for any improvement you notice and any increased interest.

Study skills are like anything else. First come the basics; then kids can get creative. Now that your kids have the note-taking skill down, they can branch out.

18 Develop Your Own Note-taking System

PARENT POINTER *Teach your kids to develop their own note-taking style.*

Admit it: Don't you have your own system when it comes to taking notes? Instead of starting a grocery list from scratch, don't you sometimes just check off a preprinted list? Or do you simply take the recipe you plan to cook to the store with you as a reminder to buy cake flour, almond extract, and chocolate chips?

Sure. We all have our own system of note-taking, and the older we get, the more fine-tuned our system is.

FYI

In truth, most adults invent their own shorthand. They use *c* for cup. On their calendar, *m* might stand for meeting; *wo* for workout, and *b* could mean birthday. Your abbreviations are as individual as you are. No one else has to understand them anyway, just as long as you do. And indeed you do. They make your life easier.

That's the valuable skill you now want to transfer to your kids, to make their lives easier too.

HELPFUL HOW-TO HINTS

SMART STARTER For that reason, tell Korbin it's time for him to come up with his own note-taking shortcuts. See what he says. Can he think of a better abbreviation besides *hw* for homework? Or *r* for reading? Or *t/F* for test on Friday?

Also explain the use of different-colored highlighters to him. For example, he can choose yellow for the main idea. Green for what he already knows. Red for what is definitely going to be on the test. At the same time, explain to Korbin what the best way is to tackle new material. And that is to PVR, which means to preview, view, and review any new lesson.

Then go on to some fun activities. Once Korbin has underlined the key ideas on a study sheet or has copied them into his notebook, according to his own shorthand system, it'll amuse him to make up a rhyme or song with the key ideas, such as:

> Juneau is the capital of Alaska;
> Lincoln is the capital of Nebraska.

After that, let Korbin work on Montana and Indiana.

Next to come will be Korbin's rap on the major countries of the world and their capitals. He'll use a world map; all you have to do is clap.

SUPER STARTER Katelyn, who is older, will branch out even more with the colored markers. She might affix squiggles and curlicues to her notes, each indicating something only she knows. Let her. Soon, she'll find out that shortcuts, not adornments, save time.

While you're admiring her newly colorful notebooks and folders, tell her about automatically numbering a clean sheet of paper when her teacher says, Today we're going to learn ten new terms. Also teach her just to read the summary of a chapter, when she is in a hurry, and copy down key words. Or glance at the discussion questions at the end of the chapter, jot down unknown terms, and then go back and read for the details.

When Katelyn's finished with her homework, but before putting her books aside for the evening, show her how to circle the three most important concepts she learned that day, and then glance at them again before going to school the next morning, so they will be fresh on her mind when the new lesson begins.

Finally, ask her to set aside some space in the back of her notebook for definitions or topics she doesn't yet grasp fully or is unsure about. Call that her trouble-spot section and help her find supplemental information on those pesky topics at home. Buy extra study materials or get them from the teacher or library, hand them to Katelyn, and watch her put her new and improved note-taking skills to work.

Celebrate with Katelyn as she deletes more and more troublesome topics from the back of her notebook. What a sense of achievement she will have!

Notes & Quotes

_____

_____

_____

No doubt about it: Kids love to make progress in school. They want to become smarter, and yours surely will.

While your kids now take pride in their notes, which will make studying for tests so much easier, they also need to know that, just as their notes can differ, so can the way different teachers present information. Isn't it important for your kids to be able to recognize the various teaching styles they might be exposed to? You bet.

Only if your kids understand what type of teaching style their teacher uses will they get the most out of a lesson. Let's make sure to give them that skill next.

19 Know the Different Teaching Styles

PARENT POINTER *Teach your kids the various teaching styles.*

Think back for a moment and remember all the teachers you had in elementary school, middle school, high school, and college. Probably no two were alike in their teaching methods. Some of your teachers started talking from the moment the bell rang. Others believed in "learning by doing" and let you work though various assignments yourself, giving instruction only when needed. Still other teachers, the rare ones, let you plan your own course of study to some degree, and then allowed you to set out and conquer the material.

FYI

Think of a workshop you attended recently. Or the latest staff meeting. Each time you had either a presenter or a superior explain or lecture to you on information they thought you needed. Another time you were given a problem to work out with your colleagues, and all the presenter did was to introduce the topics. Then you and your co-workers went to work. Still another time, new company goals or deadlines were announced, and then you were turned loose to meet them.

School can be like that at times too, but in all likelihood not all the time. Although each teaching approach has many good points, important, timeless concepts are best taught the old-fashioned way, especially during the elementary and middle-school years.

HELPFUL HOW-TO HINTS

SMART STARTER No matter which teaching style Jasmine's teacher leans toward, it's good to know what to expect. That's easy to find out at the first meeting with the teacher, during which you will probably receive some written guidelines.

Slowly read those handouts over with Jasmine and take special notice of what the teacher expects from your daughter. Are there projects listed? Is the number of book reports stated? Are there class rules? If not, ask.

Next, question Jasmine at supper about what went on in school each day. Did the teacher mainly stand in front of the class, demonstrate a math problem on the chalkboard, and then have the students work the next seven problems? That's a more traditional teaching approach, which Jasmine can easily adapt to with your help. It means all Jasmine has to do is focus on the teacher.

Or did the teacher split the class into groups of four right away and, after explaining the task, have the kids work on the problems in groups, and ask a "speaker" up to the board to present the group's answers? That's a different method of getting a lesson across and may need watching, because it can let some students fall by the wayside. In some group-work settings, only the most outgoing kids get attention; the quieter ones may not get called on. If Jasmine is shy, be sure she has extra occasions to shine at home and help her learn to assert herself more with her peers.

Or maybe the lesson plan revolves around independent-study units, which allow kids to move at their own speed. Again, that can have some drawbacks. If Jasmine is a steady, conscientious, but slow worker, she may get penalized for not advancing as fast as her quicker, more careless classmates. In this case, she may need to bring more work home. Help Jasmine catch up and maybe even work ahead at home.

SUPER STARTER

Jarrett, who is older, may have teachers with various teaching styles throughout his school day. It's best to question him about every subject and then point out the potential pitfalls of the less traditional teachers. While they often allow kids to have more fun in class, they can also reinforce weaknesses in students. So if Jarrett does lots of group work and projects, check at home, textbook in hand, to see how well he's getting the basics.

Any time you feel he's missing out on some of the basic concepts in his book, sit down with him and put him on an independent-study program at home. He'll benefit from both—the fun lessons at school and the fundamental lessons at home.

But no matter what teaching styles seem to be in vogue at Jarrett's school this year, always communicate freely with his teachers. Be open-minded and glad that schools have changed since you attended them. Be excited over the addition of computer-taught lessons and other techno methods. As long as Jarrett has you standing by with additional learning strategies, he can't go wrong.

Once Jarrett's first report card for the year comes out, look carefully at his grades. Any marks that are below an A signal challenges for Jarrett (and you, his special tutor). Sit down with Jarrett and discuss his grades with him, one by one, and make a plan for improvement together. Let him choose the subject he wants to tackle first as the one to work on next. Let him write out his plan for raising his test scores and then supervise him as he goes after his new goals. And, of course, inform his teachers about the new plans, so they'll know what's going on.

Finally, ask Jarrett's teachers about their policy for extra credit, redoing work, and retaking tests. Just like teaching styles, methods for make-up work also vary from teacher to teacher. Yet most teachers are extremely flexible and very grateful to have the parents involved. Also, at the next PTA meeting, make it a point to talk to the moms or dads of Jarrett's classmates who are making grades significantly higher than your son. Ask them for some extra tricks of the trade. Share your ideas for motivating Jarrett, and they will share their hints. You will find that parents all over are thrilled to exchange tips on raising their kids to be tops.

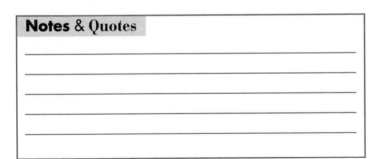

Notes & Quotes

All it takes is persistence and dedication to help your kids sail successfully across the various instructional seas they face.

That's what you have: persistence and dedication. Schools these days are more complex than they used to be, but you welcome challenges. You simply give your kids your best efforts.

What next? Next is a closer look at the kids in our classrooms today. How come some of them only lounge and linger year after year, while others lap up new learning each and every day and leap to the top of the academic heap? How do they do that? By becoming active students.

20 | Be an Active Student

PARENT POINTER *Teach your kids to be good students.*

Picture yourself walking through the mall. You can amble along for hours, glancing at the many merchandise displays and wonderful wares offered but not buying a single thing. After a while you might drag home with a headache and wonder where the time went.

Or you can come in with a nice list and a plan, jump directly into the fray, even during the most hectic preholiday shopping time, and emerge three hours later with every item marked off your list, some already colorfully gift-wrapped, and—voilà!—all done for the season.

FYI

The same situation can be true for students. Some merely show up in school every day and meander aimlessly through their schedules. Having learned no new skills, they drag home when school is over and flop on the couch, with the TV flickering or the radio blaring, and complain that school was bor-ing.

In contrast, other students do 99 percent of their learning during class time. Then they have only a little to do at home, which leaves them time for some advanced study. On top of that, they're enjoying themselves. TV? Radio? Sure, but *Turn it down or turn it off* is their motto during the week.

So, to what group do your kids belong? To what group do you want them to belong? For that always comes first, your making up your mind about what you expect from your kids. And, naturally, you expect the best.

HELPFUL HOW-TO HINTS

SMART STARTER Ask Anthony to get actively involved in class. That means pay very close attention to the teacher, and stay alert during the whole day. For that he needs plenty of sleep the night before, plus a good breakfast and a great lunch. See to it that he always has them.

Next, ask his teacher if Anthony is tired during the day, or if his mind seems to wander. In that case, move his bedtime up an hour, cut back on TV watching and video games, and increase the time he gets to play outside with his new puppy.

After a week, check to see how much Anthony's attention span has increased and be sure to comment on it. Post whatever positive note(s) the teacher sends home on the fridge, and write one of your own to display too. *Good work, Anthony!*

Also, find out what classes he enjoys most and get him even more involved with those. If Anthony likes math, skim his math book and prepare him at home so he'll be ready to respond if his teacher talks about fractions or dividends.

Let Anthony's test scores, graded homework, and work sheets be your guide. If they are all outstanding, he is an active student. If his scores are low or indicate incomplete work, get in touch with the teacher again and find out where the problem is. If Anthony has a tendency to rush through his work, teach him to slow down. While you're supervising his homework, tell him to stop and think while he's working, repeat what he's reading in his own words, and ask himself if he understands what he is working on. Becoming an active student is a journey with stops and starts. You'll need to help Anthony get going again and again.

SUPER STARTER

As for Anna, who is older, ask her always to glance at the board at the end of the class to make sure she hasn't forgotten to copy all the important facts. Teach her to ask for clarification during a lesson or at the end. In her textbook, the headings in bold print and the summaries provide quick additional data. Let Anna choose a special reward for herself if and when her teachers notice any increased attention span and participation in class.

Like all kids, Anna needs structure. So let her post her homework hours. Of course, you'll add on more work if Anna doesn't have enough to do. Tell her she can select a different subject for every day of the week and choose what she'll concentrate on. Let her also decide on what consequences should be in place if she doesn't become a more active student.

Teach Anna to avoid daydreaming in class by forcing herself to write down something every minute, or by formulating questions on what the topic in class is. Teach her how to outline her teacher's lecture. On the left side of her notebook page she can jot down the anticipated outline. On the right hand, she can copy the teacher's actual outline. Additionally, teach Anna to cut back on her doodling. Once she counts each time she's looking out the window or watching the clock in class, she can then set a goal for herself to reduce those time-wasting activities.

When Anna is doing homework, let her count down the number of tough pages she has to study in the following manner:

> *Only ten, tell me when,*
> *Only nine, and I'll be fine,*
> *Only eight, that's so great,*
> *Only seven, and I'll be in heaven,*
> *Only six, I'm out of the sticks,*
> *Only five, I'll come alive,*
> *Only four, then no more,*
> *Only three, then I'm free,*
> *Only two, and I'll be through,*
> *Only one, and I'm all done. Ta-da!*

As she finishes each page, she should pause and review what she's learned. That surely will break up any long assignment and make it more fun.

Notes & Quotes
_____
_____
_____
_____
_____

And, Mom or Dad, while you're working hard to turn your kids into more active students, don't forget to become more active parents. That means you're staying close by while they're studying. No interruptions allowed, so turn the phone off.

Meet their teachers as soon as possible. Of course, you'll tell them about your children's strengths, attend parent-teacher conferences, keep a notebook on your communications with the school, and thank the teachers for their good work. Finally, write a letter of commendation for all the help you're being given.

Once your kids are active students, they deserve a present, which you will be thrilled to give them. It's a special present, a huge gift that will change their lives forever. Curious? Read on.

Part V: Reading Smarts

Help your kids to . . .
love reading

One of the most special gifts anyone can give us is the love of reading. Can there be anything more enjoyable than to relax with a good book? Yet too many kids are denied that joy.

Nothing is more crucial to school success. So let's not waste another minute. Mark Twain said, "The man who does not read books has no advantage over the one who cannot read." To that let's add, Why not make reading your kids' foremost hobby? The benefits are incredible. Just let the following top teacher tips guide you.

TOP TIP
21 Enjoy Reading

PARENT POINTER *Teach your kids to love reading.*

How much do you read? Is it only work-related material, or do you read for fun and relaxation too? Do you have favorite authors whose new books you anticipate with eagerness? Is reading a favorite form of relaxation?

FYI

Without a love for reading, much schoolwork is just plain tough for kids. That's why so many students find school boring-boring-boring—because they can't read fluently. They have to struggle with every textbook that's put in front of them. This struggle gets harder the higher they move through the grades. Academic success is simply out of reach for kids who always have to labor over their reading assignments. Those students who are continuously afraid to get called on to read aloud soon learn to hate school.

But that doesn't include your kids. From here on out, you will make reading their number one hobby. How? It's easy. Just turn reading into a favorite family pastime.

HELPFUL HOW-TO HINTS

SMART STARTER Just as you supervise Jana's brushing her teeth every evening, now add thirty minutes of reading to her bedtime ritual. Make sure no interruptions spoil the fun as you read a book to her that she has picked out. When that book's finished, let her choose another, but this time alternate. You read one paragraph, she reads the next. During the day make comments about the nightly reading. Tell Jana you can't wait for your next book session. Ask her questions about what she remembers and let her predict the outcome of the story at hand.

In a short while, you will find her wanting to read ahead on her own. Good, let her. Just make sure there are always more books at your house, so she has a goal. Her school librarian will give you a list of books that have won either the Caldecott Medal (for illustrations) or the Newbery Medal (for story). Have Jana check out some of those books and read them. Then have her tell you what she read on her own before you start your usual bedtime team reading.

After several weeks, just sit with her as she reads silently in bed. Bring your own book and read your favorite author. Afterward, exchange summaries of what you each read.

For variety, include other printed materials. Subscribe to a children's magazine for Jana and, while she reads hers, you can delve into *Newsweek* or *Time*.

SUPER STARTER Jake, who is older, is interested in trains, so get him five books on trains and watch him become absorbed by the material. You can sit in his room with him while he reads or just check on him every so often. But he should read a minimum of thirty minutes every evening. More than likely, once he's gotten used to the idea, he'll read even longer.

After he's finished all the train books, get out his school's reading list and have him choose his next selection from that list. Then have him alternate: one book from the list, then one he's picked out. Also do some research and find out which classics Jake's school librarian recommends. Then select Monday evening to read aloud together—perhaps *Treasure Island*. Each of you can choose two paragraphs or whatever suits you.

After every five books Jake has read, plan for a reward, perhaps a special outing just for you and him. And before he tackles the next five books, let him pick another treat in advance. He can list the treat on a reading record on the fridge.

Another day, have a speed-reading contest. Choose two chapters of equal length and read one silently while Jake times you. He reads the other while you time him. Afterward teach him some reading shortcuts, like focusing on names, places, dates.

Before starting a more difficult book, do a little research to find out its background or have Jake look up the state or country where the action takes place. Then have him quiz you on what he found out. Kids enjoy being smart. During the summer or vacation time, have a read-a-thon with Jake. See if he can read more books than you in a given time.

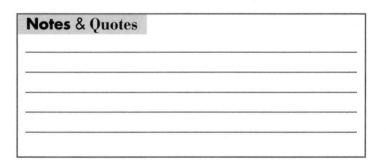

There are many ways your kids can share their joy of reading. They can read a story to day-care kids, become reading volunteers at the retirement center down the street, or read to kids who are hospitalized by offering to be their book buddies.

Then stand back and observe. Notice how much joy you made possible for your kids when you showed them, by word and deed, how to love reading. And believe me, that love of reading won't just bring up your kids' reading scores. It will also lead to the improvement of other important school skills.

We live in a hurried world. Often we just want to cut to the chase. Hey, don't bother me with the details, is our attitude; just give me the bottom line.

In reading, the bottom line is comprehension. Do your kids quickly understand what they read? If not, let's show them how.

TOP TIP 22

Learn to Comprehend and Summarize

PARENT POINTER *Teach your kids how better to comprehend and summarize.*

When you're reading, do you ever find yourself staring at the same page or paragraph for a long time, not knowing what you have just read, and then have to go back over the same lines to get the information you need? This happens to all of us, especially when we're stressed out and are reading aimlessly. But I bet it doesn't happen when you know you will be asked questions on the text later. Or when a raise at work depends on it.

FYI

Just think of how much time could be saved all over the world if people could be taught to comprehend what they read the first time around. How many mistakes could be avoided! We could all be so much more productive. It's that increased productivity you want your kids to have. Let me show you how to accomplish it.

HELPFUL HOW-TO HINTS

SMART STARTER The trick to great reading comprehension is to teach Zack five little words, which are: Who? When? What? Where? Why? From now on, when you read a story with him, ask him those W's:

Who is this story talking about?

When did it happen?

What happened to the main character?

Where is it happening?

Why(or how) does it happen?

After Zack gives you the answers to those questions, ask him to make up a short talk about the story and include those answers. That's a summary. That's all there is to it.

From then on, teach Jake to read with the W-words in mind. If he can't answer the questions, he isn't paying attention to what he's reading. Tell him to be a detective and scout out the answers as quickly as possible.

Practice this skill over and over with him by reading to him and helping him find the answers, then using the information in three or four sentences. You show him how it's done, then have him repeat the process.

Before Jake goes to school next time, be sure he has the five questions memorized. He can use the fingers of one hand as a reminder. Then when he comes home, ask him about something he read and see if he used his new detective skills. Can he tell you the main facts in a short summary?

SUPER STARTER Ask Zarah, who has the five W's down pat, to summarize a story in three sentences, using the answers to each one of the questions. Then help her squeeze all that information into one long sentence, which will have both of you laughing as you delete unnecessary words. Then tell her to send a pretend telegram about the book she is reading now. Can she shorten a summary that much and still get all the information across?

Next say, "Janet, 1891, lost horse, island, storm" and ask her what kind of story she would write if she used all these five facts. Then discuss with her how *you* would approach such a story.

Move on to newspaper and magazine articles and let Zarah quickly give you the main details, plus a brief summary, using complete sentences.

Another time, ask her to write the lyrics to a song based on the gist of the history chapter she's studying at the moment. Only one requirement: Her song must include the answers to the five W's.

Also teach her to pause after reading a complicated selection and ask herself: What would I include on a Web site devoted to this? What else besides the five W's is important here?

Notes & Quotes

_____

_____

_____

_____

_____

To further encourage your kids' comprehending and summarizing skills, have them keep a fact file for each book they have read. Make up some index cards for them with the five questions already printed on them. Then, each time they read a new chapter, they can fill in the facts. To do this, they will have to pay more attention to what they read. And when it's time to study for a test, all they have to do is review their file and maybe make up some multiple-choice questions about the chapters.

What an increase in reading comprehension! What fun your kids will have, flipping through their cards. What a feeling of pride they will experience!

With each new reading selection or book your kids master, they will add to their storehouse of knowledge. Then, when they need to prove what they know, all they have to do is go into their mental storehouse and pull out what's needed.

To prove they know their material, kids are often asked to look at two selections or two books, lay them side by side mentally, and judge them. How does one measure up against the other? For your kids to answer that question efficiently, they need to learn the next skill.

23 Learn to Compare and Contrast

PARENT POINTER *Teach your kids to compare and contrast.*

We make judgments every day. Whether we compare the price of strawberries to that of blueberries and finally decide to buy the purple plums instead, to add more fruit to our diets, or whether we comparison-shop for a new stove, we judge one item against the merits of one or more other items. This skill is vital. It helps us make the best use of our money and empowers us to take charge of our lives.

FYI

Kids need that same skill in school, but in a more abstract way. They need to be able to discuss intelligently the contributions of two presidents or the discoveries of two scientists. To accomplish that, they need to know that *comparison* means looking for similarities and *contrast* means looking for differences. Then they need a way to do both, systematically and proficiently. Here is a simple blueprint as to how that is done.

HELPFUL HOW-TO HINTS

SMART STARTER Show Sallie two of her toys, her favorite stuffed dog and her special pillow, and ask her what they have in common and what makes them different. Let her name three similarities and three differences.

Next, ask her to write a paragraph about the similarities (both toys are hers, soft, and cuddly, perhaps). Later, ask her to write a paragraph about the differences (they're different in color, size, and cost, for example).

Then practice the comparison-contrast skill with Sallie using other items in the house. Advance to people she knows, and then to activities, like sports.

After Sallie finishes a book, ask her to compare and contrast it with another book. This time let her name five similarities and five differences, or as many as she can come up with. Also tell her that with books you can "specialize," which means you can just focus on the stories or the authors or the outside appearance of the book, and so on.

Tell her that the purpose of this skill is to come to a final conclusion based on facts. What's her conclusion in regards to those two books? Which one would she recommend to her cousin? Which one wouldn't she recommend? Why?

SUPER STARTER Saylor, who is older, can tell you all about which books he likes and which he doesn't, but when it comes to specifics he may shrug. Teach him some basic literary terms, such as *fiction* (a made-up story), *nonfiction* (a story that really happened), *plot* (the action), *characters* (the people in the story), and *setting* (the time and place in which the action occurs). Now he has something to compare and contrast.

Post a simple outline for Saylor, that he'll soon memorize, which is:

> Paragraph one: s1, s2, s3 (write three sentences about the similarities)

Paragraph two: d1, d2, d3 (write three sentences about the differences)

Paragraph three: conclusion

If Saylor wants to be more creative, he can try this outline:

Paragraph one: s1, d1 (write one sentence about a similarity and one about a difference)

Paragraph two: s2, d2 (write a second sentence about another similarity and one about another difference)

Paragraph three: conclusion

Next, point out to Saylor that research is often the only way to have enough facts to make valid comparisons. Let him pick a topic, turn him loose, and watch him check out all the good and bad points, perhaps of various brands of mountain bikes, one of which he wants you to buy him for his birthday. Then tell him to give you a talk on what he has researched. Better yet, have him write you an essay on what he found out.

That will lead to your introducing him to a list of most valuable phrases, such as:

on the one hand	on the other hand
in contrast	consequently
furthermore	moreover
nevertheless	otherwise
therefore	yet
similarly	in the same manner
as a consequence	thus
in summary	finally
all points considered	in conclusion

This list is a lifesaver for anyone writing essays, especially comparative ones.

Last, ask Saylor to apply his new skills when he discusses new movies, videos, or the hottest techno toys. Prod him a little to get him to cite specifics, and always have him examine not only the advantages of something but the disadvantages as well, as compared and contrasted to other items.

Notes & Quotes

_____

_____

_____

_____

_____

This skill will not only help your kids get top grades on their compositions and discussions, it will also help them make good choices in life. And that's what making your kids smarter is *really* all about.

Now we come to something else your kids need, something they can always count on and refer to, a specific piece of knowledge—in other words, a simple, solid standard against which other items can be judged or measured.

What simple, solid scholastic standard can you give your kids? In school, it is a piece of writing that has been recognized as having lasting and significant value over the years, generation after generation.

24 | Know One Piece of Writing Well

PARENT POINTER *Teach your kids to know at least one literary work well.*

Look into your closet right now. Don't you have one outfit that's always right, always ready, kept just for that occasion when you need to look extra presentable? Sure you do. You have one good suit or dress that always pulls you through, right?

Well, your kids need to own something similar to be tops in school, something they can rely on in most class situations, either as a basis for a discussion or a jumping-off point for research or simply as a memory jogger. And that something is knowing a classic.

FYI

A *classic* is a piece of writing that does triple duty:

1. It opens kids' eyes to the whole world.

2. It teaches them about mankind's hopes, beliefs, and history.

3. It tends to uplift and improve those who read it.

Besides being beautifully written, with a vocabulary that challenges kids, a classic often has a powerful message and makes us into better people because it causes us to think, encourages us to understand, and helps us to try again and again. How do you get your kids to fall in love with a classic?

HELPFUL HOW-TO HINTS

SMART STARTER Ask Eric's teacher for a list of classics, read several of them with him, and ask him which is his favorite.

When he has picked one, help him learn as much as possible about his selection. Have him look up the author and write a short biography, an account of the writer's life. Help him to identify the various literary terms (plot, characters, setting) in the story and write the information on index cards. Post the cards on the bulletin board in his room so he has them as a guide.

If Eric can't find a classic he really likes, steer him toward animal stories. While he's reading them, introduce him to *Aesop's Fables*. These stories are short, and he can easily choose one or two to study further.

Next, help Eric look up some background on this Greek storyteller and explain to him what a *fable* is (a story that makes a point about human beings or teaches a lesson while using animals and allowing them to speak and act like people).

In the end, maybe Eric will like best Aesop's fable about the boy who cried wolf. The lesson in this story is that liars will not be believed even when they tell the truth. Can Eric relate this lesson to an experience of his own?

SUPER STARTER With your older child, Erica, explain how great it is for kids to know one classic story really well that can always serve as a standby, a written selection that can do heavy duty in school each and every time it's needed. Then ask her if she knows such a story. If she does, examine that story with her to see if it measures up. (See 1, 2, and 3 in FYI.)

To be able to judge a story, Erica needs to know the following literary terms:

> plot (story line)
>
> characters
>
> protagonist (hero or heroine)
>
> antagonist (villain)
>
> high point or climax
>
> setting (time and place)
>
> myth (legend)
>
> biography (a person's life described by someone else)
>
> autobiography (life story written by that person)
>
> fiction (made-up story)
>
> nonfiction (true story)

If Erica knows a story with classic qualities, give her a note card and have her copy some of these literary terms and then fill in the information. If she doesn't know any such classic, introduce her to the famous work "The Necklace" by Guy de Maupassant. In this fictional short story, the poor heroine desperately wants to attend a lavish party and borrows a fabulous diamond necklace to impress everyone. When she loses the necklace, she slaves for the next ten years to pay for it, only to learn in the end that the necklace was fake.

If Erica prefers stories that are true, read with her the well-known nonfiction selection "The Secret Room." This story details how the author, Corrie ten Boom, heroically built a secret room within her bedroom to hide several fleeing Jews from the Nazis.

Whatever classic story Erica picks to focus on, be sure to have her point out what makes it a classic and what kids the world over could learn from it. It's in the course of this discussion that Erica will learn to distinguish between good, timeless literature and less valuable writings that might be labeled junk.

This is an important lesson, because the ability to distinguish between good and poor quality, no matter what the items, is priceless. Soon Erica will be able to apply that same skill when it comes to movies, TV shows, and magazines.

Alert and critical, she'll know what's terrific and what's trash.

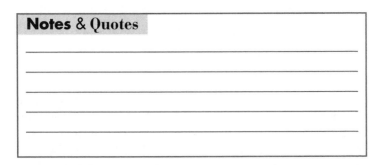

Notes & Quotes

In your workplace, is one terrific outfit really all you need? Of course not. Similarly, your kids need to know other masterpieces, other examples of the greatness of the world. That greatness can easily be found in the works of the world's best authors. Who are they?

25 Know Something About World Literature

PARENT POINTER *Teach your kids about world literature.*

Think about the whole world, the various places you've visited or would like to visit someday. Isn't it fascinating how many different nations there are? (Several hundred, according to one source.) All those various countries and cultures! How many different languages are spoken? (Also several hundred, according to another source.)

Which of those languages are spoken by the largest number of people?

Here are the first ten languages, in descending order: Chinese, Spanish, English, Bengali, Hindi, Portuguese, Russian, Japanese, German, and Korean.

FYI

Of course, few people have the chance to visit all the countries in which those languages are spoken, let alone have the time and energy to study all those different tongues. But with the help of books, you and your kids can do the next best thing: You can sample some great books from various regions of the world. You don't need to get on a plane. You don't need to study foreign language tapes. All you have to do is avail yourself of a few English translations of the best works of foreign authors, and you can experience their splendor. Then present a selection to your kids.

HELPFUL HOW-TO HINTS

SMART STARTER Open a world map and ask Deidre to find the United States. You may have to help her. Then give her a sheet of tracing paper and have her trace its outline. What country is to the north? (Canada.) And which lies to the south? (Mexico.)

Buy a globe and show her the great landmasses of the earth: North America, South America, Europe, Africa, Asia, Australia, and Antarctica. Tell her that each continent has many countries, in which people live just like you, and these people have kids who go to school and read books, just like Deidre.

Have Deidre name all the countries she's heard of and help her find them on the globe or on a map. Help her locate the capitals of those countries, plus a few new ones.

Next, ask her teacher for a list of foreign books she recommends for Deidre. Let your daughter choose a book and check it out of the library and then read it with her, after finding the country on the map and getting some background information on it.

Spin the globe, or have Deidre pick another country using any method she likes. This time research what kids in this particular country are reading in school and then read those books to, or with, Deidre. Talk about them and compare them with what Deidre is reading in class at the moment.

From now on, any time Deidre mentions a foreign city, such as Paris or Moscow, help her find a French or Russian author and expose her to literature from that country, even if it's just a paragraph or two. Good idea? *Oui* or *non? Nyet?*

SUPER STARTER Devon, who is older, probably has classmates from various ethnic backgrounds. Ask him about them, help him print out a world map with the help of the computer, and show him how to pinpoint the countries of origin of his classmates or their parents.

Next, ask Devon to research the Nobel Prize winners for literature of the last hundred years and print out a list of them for his bulletin board. From that list he may want to choose an outstanding writer from a foreign country that interests him. Let's say he's fascinated by Australia. He'll look up Patrick White, the winner for 1973, from Australia. Or if Devon is fascinated by Japan, he'll check out Kenzaburo Oe, the winner for 1994, from Japan.

Ask Devon's teacher or librarian for suggestions of books dealing with, or written by, Australian or Japanese writers.

If Devon can't decide where to start, teach him a little about—or read up with him on—the lives and works of the following Nobel Prize winners:

> Boris Pasternak (U.S.S.R., 1958)
>
> Pablo Neruda (Chile, 1971)
>
> Naguib Mahfouz (Egypt, 1988)
>
> Toni Morrison (U.S., 1993).

These aren't authors who write for kids, but they are authors of world renown, and to know them will inspire Devon.

Last, choose some poems by writers that Devon has never heard of. Maybe something written by Native Americans will speak to you; here's your chance to share it with your son. He might like this poem by a Winnebago Indian:

> *Beautiful it looked, this newly created world.*
> *Along the entire length and breadth of Grandmother Earth*
> *extended the green reflection of her covering,*
> *and the escaping odors were pleasant to inhale.*

Or maybe you have found a short story that puzzles you or a science fiction piece that astounds you. Read it first, then ask Devon to read it. You can discuss it over dinner. There won't be any time to focus on what Devon's done wrong recently; there will only be time to talk about what's going on in his mind, which is expanding.

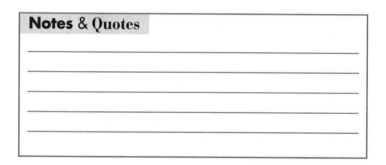

Notes & Quotes

As you widen your literary horizons, you will help your kids do the same. And as you expose them to outstanding writers from all around the world, always ask your kids for their opinion. Do they like this foreign writer or that one? Why or why not? Ask them to look through an anthology of foreign authors, which you check out, until they come across a selection they definitely like. In that way, they will travel all around the world mentally. And back or forward in time.

Oh, yes. Have them—if only for the time it takes to read about it—live in another century or another country and experience the joys and sorrows of other ethnic groups or nationalities. Live vicariously during harsher times. In other words, have your kids really think about other people and their problems. This will help them develop empathy for people from all walks of life and all corners of the earth. You gave your kids life, didn't you? Now give them wisdom and understanding and a global outlook. Make the world theirs.

You're already halfway through these fifty top teacher tips. By investing your extra time, you're getting great returns. And the returns are compounded because when you make your kids smarter, you're also making *their* kids smarter. And their kids will be smarter too, and so on. All because of what you're teaching your kids today.

So keep it up. Keep building your kids' school skills.

Part VI: Writing Smarts

Help your kids to . . .
become good writers

Now that you've made sure that your kids love to read, it's time to provide them with the next superb skill, the ability to write well. Being able to write well is terribly important. So much of what we learn can only be tested by the way we show our knowledge, and that is through the words we put on paper. Knowing something in school without being able to demonstrate it in written form means little. But being able to show proficiency on a sheet of paper, whether in a short but terrific paragraph or in a longer, well-thought-out essay—that's the key to top grades. Teachers cannot read what's in your kids' minds, but they can easily read what shows up in their notebooks, homework papers, book reports, and tests.

26 Write Good Sentences

PARENT POINTER *Teach your kids to write good sentences.*

First impressions are very important. Whether we apply for a job, face a new customer, interview a child caregiver, or present ourselves to a person in authority, that first meeting often sets the tone for the next meeting—or decides whether there will even be a next one. So making a good *first* impression is crucial. We never get a second chance to do it.

FYI

This is even more true for kids in school, because the first-impression scenario happens over and over. Every time they move up a grade, they get another chance to make a good first impression on one or more new teachers. So from day one, kids need to look and act presentable, plus they need one more important skill: the ability to write a good solid sentence. That's the way they introduce themselves best to their new instructors. Let's make sure they can do it.

HELPFUL HOW-TO HINTS

SMART STARTER First ask Brian, What is a sentence? He'll probably say, "A bunch of words." And you'll say, Almost, but not quite. Then you'll explain that a sentence is some words that follow a pattern. That is, a sentence must be a complete thought. It always has a subject (who or what the sentence talks about) and a verb (what who or what does).

Then ask Brian, How do you feel? He'll probably say, "Sleepy." Say, Good, but that's just a fragment. Can you put that into a complete sentence? Tell me who is sleepy. And Brian will say, "I am sleepy." All right! That's a complete sentence.

The next step is to call out some nouns (persons, places, or things), such as cat, mouse, Popsicle, and restaurant, and ask Brian to make complete sentences with them. He may say,

> The cat is naughty.
>
> The mouse is hungry.
>
> The Popsicle is yummy.
>
> The restaurant is pretty cool.

Well done! Now call out some verbs (action words or forms of *to be*), such as play, skip, is, and munch, and ask Brian to make complete sentences with those verbs. He will perhaps say:

> I play.
>
> This ball skips.
>
> My brother is smart.
>
> A little rabbit was munching on a nice carrot.

Again, well done! Finally, give Brian a sheet of paper and ask him to write sentences with the following words: dog, spell, turkey, hum, Billy. Then it's your turn. Write a paragraph, including several full sentences and several fragments, and have Brian pick out the complete sentences and tell you why they are complete. Then have him add some words to the fragments to make them into complete sentences too.

SUPER STARTER Brianna is older and already knows about sentences. She needs to learn about the many ways sentences can be classified. Ask her to give you a sentence for each of the following four types:

1. Declarative (makes a statement: My friends and I love cheese pizza.)
2. Interrogative (asks a question: What's your favorite food?)
3. Imperative (states a command: Stop chewing so fast.)
4. Exclamatory (expresses strong feelings: What a delicious pizza!)

Next explain the importance of knowing the parts of speech, so Brianna can become a master of sentence writing and have an easier time studying a foreign language. The eight parts of speech are

1. noun (person, place, or thing: *house*)
2. pronoun (takes the place of a noun: *it*)
3. verb (tells of an action or state of being: *stands*)
4. adverb (modifies verb, adjective, or another adverb: *grandly*)
5. adjective (describes noun or pronoun: *huge*)
6. conjunction (connects words or phrases: *and*)
7. interjection (expresses a strong emotion, uses exclamation point: *Oh!*)
8. preposition (relates one word to another: *in*)

Now, focus on the two most important parts of speech, nouns and verbs. Nouns can be *common* (naming persons, places, or things in general) or *proper* (naming individual persons, places, or things). Proper nouns are always capitalized. Verbs also are of two main types, *transitive* (action) verbs and *intransitive* (state of being) verbs. Ask Brianna what kinds of verbs follow below:

> paint: I painted my chair. (transitive/action)
>
> look: My father looked good. (intransitive/state of being)
>
> pace: After the test my sister paced the floor. (transitive/action)
>
> are: Our geraniums are bright red. (intransitive/state of being)
>
> drive: I can't wait to drive a car. (transitive/action)

Once Brianna has a feel for nouns and verbs, let her have fun with them. When she mentions any object from now on, ask her for a *synonym* for it, a word with the same meaning. Should she say *dress*, ask her to name other words meaning the same thing (garment, clothes, outfit, skirt and top, gown, frock). And if she should say *walk*, play the game with her and both of you come up alternately with traipse, amble, stroll, saunter, skip, mosey, prance, dance, step, strut, swagger, shuffle, trudge, wade, waddle, trail, mince, tiptoe, and toddle. The more nouns and verbs Brianna knows, the better her sentences will be.

Finally, teach Brianna the following three basic sentence proofreading skills:

1. Always make sure the subject and verb agree.

> *Incorrect*: The schedule for classes are posted on the door.

Correct: The schedule for classes is posted on the door.

2. Never use a run-on sentence or comma splice.

Incorrect: Bailey wants to become a librarian she loves books.

Incorrect: Bailey wants to become a librarian, she loves books.

Correct: Bailey wants to become a librarian. She loves books.

Correct: Bailey wants to become a librarian because she loves books.

3. Make sure every sentence begins with a capital letter and ends with a punctuation mark.

Incorrect: the bus swerved and stopped suddenly

Correct: The bus swerved and stopped suddenly.

Notes & Quotes

_____

_____

_____

_____

_____

Being to able to write a good sentence is like having good building blocks forever at one's disposal. Who can construct a sturdy structure out of broken brick? Nobody. To build a solid structure you need good building blocks, intact materials. The same is true for writing.

A great sentence is a crucial requirement for what comes next, a structure of sentences known as a paragraph. Good paragraphs are easy once your kids know how to write good sentences. All they have to do is write one good sentence after another. Let's make sure your kids can handle that.

27 | Write Good Paragraphs

PARENT POINTER *Teach your kids to write a*
good paragraph.

Wouldn't it be great if you could guarantee your kids that
they would always make good grades, especially in any class
where they are required to write, which is most of them?
Well, now you can.

All you have to do is make sure they master the paragraph,
which is the most frequently asked-for school assignment.
Even in longer writing, the paragraph is key, since even the
lengthiest essays, book reports, and term papers are only so
many paragraphs, one after another. If your kids can dash off a
solid paragraph or two on whatever topic is at hand, they can
do their homework assignments more efficiently, get higher
test scores on essay tests, and feel more comfortable in all their
classes, whether it's language, social studies, or science.

FYI

All your kids really need to know is what, besides good sentences, it takes to compose a good paragraph.

First, know what a paragraph is. A paragraph is a group of
sentences that all deal with the same idea.

Second, know how a paragraph begins. A paragraph
begins with a topic sentence, which states the main idea
(theme). Then come more sentences.

Third, and most important, know that all sentences in a paragraph are related to each other, just like people. Aren't we all related to another person in some way? Sure. Similarly, ideas are related, especially those in a paragraph.

There are four basic idea relationships in paragraphs: time order, comparison/contrast, cause and effect, and simple listing. Here are examples of each.

1. Time order

Read the following paragraph:

> During our first week in Finland, we visited Helsinki. After that, we took a bus north to see the countryside. Later we stopped at several of the many picturesque lakes. Finally we went on a cross-country hike through a huge forest of birch trees.

Do you see how the details in this paragraph are related in *time order*? Expressions like "during our first week," "after that," "later," and "finally" are the clues.

2. Comparison/contrast

Look at the next paragraph:

> On our trip to Finland, we enjoyed the lake visits and the hike through the birch woods much more than our short stop in Helsinki. The outdoors adventures were entirely different from what we were used to in the United States, while Helsinki, although very majestic, was just another big city to us.

Do you see how two experiences (lake visits, hike through the woods) are compared with one (Helsinki)? The writer is making a contrast between them. The expressions "much more than" and "entirely different from" are clues. This kind of idea relationship is called *comparison/contrast*.

3. Cause and effect

Now read a third paragraph:

> Because we had seen so many areas of Finland and spent ten exciting days in that country, we began to feel almost at home there. For that reason, once back home again, we were able to notice several mistakes in Mr. Smith's talk on "Fabulous Finland."

Do you see how that paragraph expresses still another idea development, that of *cause and effect*? The trip to Finland caused an effect—the ability to recognize mistakes in Mr. Smith's lecture. Expressions like "because" and "for that reason" are clues to this type of relationship. The cause (our trip to Finland) comes first, and then comes the effect (our ability to notice mistakes), but one could also put the effect first and the cause last (We were able to find mistakes in Mr. Smith's talk because we had seen Finland firsthand).

4. Simple listing

Finally, read this paragraph:

> On our trip to Finland, we visited the old city of Helsinki and some other, less famous cities, such as Turku. We also drove to numerous picturesque lakes and hiked through some of the vast birch tree forests. Additionally, we stopped at outdoor camps and saunas and went to historic churches and gift shops.

Do you see how this paragraph gives a *simple listing* of all the places visited on the trip to Finland? Words like "also" and "additionally" are clues. But you don't find out in what order we visited the various locations, do you? Nor do you learn whether the writer liked one place better than another, or if the trip had any effect on us.

There, are of course, many other ways to develop a paragraph, but these four mentioned above are the most basic ones your kids need to know.

HELPFUL HOW-TO HINTS

SMART STARTER One morning when you're not too busy, get dressed for work but keep on one old house slipper. Then ask Gina what's wrong with your outfit. With a giggle, she'll point to the offending slipper. Right, you'll say. Then tell her you were pretending to be a paragraph. The house slipper was a sentence that didn't belong.

Next tell Gina a story about when you went to school. Suddenly veer off the topic and talk about what's going to be for supper tomorrow—tuna casserole—and then stop and ask, Which statement didn't belong in this story?

Ask Gina to tell you how she makes her bed. Say, Act as if I don't know anything about bed making and you're teaching me from scratch. Start her off with this sentence (topic sentence): "Every morning when I get up, I make my bed."

Another time ask Gina to write a paragraph with five or more sentences with this topic sentence: "The best way to make popcorn is in the microwave."

Finally, when you're reading a story with Gina, stop every so often and ask her to examine a paragraph. Find its topic sentence and the various related ideas.

SUPER STARTER Ask Gabriel, who is older, to name the four kinds of idea relationships in paragraph writing (see FYI). Teach Gabriel some of the key words frequently used in those paragraph patterns.

> time order: *first, second, third, after, then, later, last, finally*

> comparison/contrast: *but, on the other hand, in contrast, yet, however*

> cause and effect: *consequently, therefore, since, because, as a result*

> simple listing: *in addition, also, moreover, besides, furthermore, plus*

On another occasion, listen to a speech on TV with Gabriel and ask him to identify what type of idea development the speaker used. Alert Gabriel to the key words just listed.

Look through newspapers and magazines with Gabriel, find a paragraph for each of the four types, and read them aloud. Then ask him, Which type of paragraph is this? Why?

Help Gabriel write a paragraph for each method. Give him a topic ("Our Most Exciting Family Vacation" or "Dinner Out" or "My Excursion to the Mall") or let him choose one he likes.

Discuss with Gabriel some of his favorite topics. Or give him those mentioned below, and have him tell you which idea relationship would be most suitable for the topic.

> Computer games

> Sprained ankle

> My last birthday party

> Two outstanding athletes

Finally, ask him to write a great paragraph on two or three topics. Post them in his room. While he's doing that, write a paragraph yourself and post it next to his. Ask Gabriel to critique your writing. Did you begin with a topic sentence? Are all your ideas related? What idea relationship did you use?

Think of how much fun Gabriel will have dissecting your writing. Wow.

Notes & Quotes

_____

_____

_____

_____

_____

After your kids have the paragraph basics down pat, you may want to show them some of the finer points. It's one thing to swim, another to know the different strokes, right? Knowing just the dog paddle means surviving. Knowing all kinds of swimming techniques is thriving. Same with paragraph writing. Thus this question: Why limit your kids to the basic paragraph menu when there are so many wonderful varieties to explore, so many tips of the trade just waiting to be acquired, and so many quick and easy helpful hints crammed into the next pages to make paragraph writing even more enjoyable?

One quick and easy hint deals with just getting started. It helps overcome the reluctance so many kids have to pick up pen or pencil and put something on paper. It's true. Top teachers say that these days many kids complain over and over, *I just don't know how to start.* Let's solve that problem.

28 Know How to Begin a Paragraph

PARENT POINTER *Teach your kids to analyze the beginnings of paragraphs.*

Procrastination. That's something we all have to overcome. Just look at your messy hall closet, the cleaning out of which you've put off too long. But hey! That's all right. As long as you can find what you need, who cares?

Just think how great it would be if someone would invent a simple procedure to get you started, and then everything else would fall into place. All you'd have to do is pull a magic string and the biggest jumble in your house would unravel. Every item would scoot to where it belongs.

Fortunately, there is such a magic string in writing.

FYI

That magic string is the topic sentence. Since it comes first in most paragraphs, we need to examine it, discuss it, and deal with it. Then, using the strategies from the previous chapter, your kids will find that the rest of the paragraph takes care of itself.

So how do you find the magic string to pull—that is, the best topic sentence—with which to kick off a paragraph? That depends on the subject at hand, of course. Let's look at some opening sentences:

The subject I am going to write about is _____ .

It is interesting to realize that _____ .

The reason why I'm writing about this is_____ .

Webster's dictionary defines _____as _____ .

Do you like them? Not much? I agree.

It's not that these opening sentences are outrageously awful, it's just that they stall. They're hemming and hawing and not getting us any closer to the magic string, the actual topic sentence. If possible, let's ditch them. Teach your kids to start with the actual topic. Help them get to the point.

HELPFUL HOW-TO HINTS

SMART STARTER Explain to Avery that a topic sentence always states or restates the main idea he's going to write on, and it must be a complete sentence. If the assignment is "My Summer Vacation," ask Avery to call out some sentences that could serve as topic sentences. Here are two examples:

My summer vacation was the best ever.

This year my summer vacation turned into an adventure.

Have Avery name some topics that interest him, such as Tiger Woods or dinosaurs. Then you supply a topic sentence for each. Here are two possibilities:

Tiger Woods is an athlete I admire.

Ever since I can remember I have been interested in dinosaurs.

The next time you two are outside, call out some words to Avery, such as *baseball*, *lawn*, or *bird's nest*, and ask him for a topic sentence with those words. While he's thinking, offer him some possible topic sentences of your own.

After a few days, give Avery a sheet of paper, pen or pencil, and the subject *ice cream* and ask him to write a topic sentence. He may write, *My favorite ice cream is chocolate fudge with nuts*. Then ask him why and listen to all his reasons. Following that, have him choose a subject, and both of you write a topic sentence and the rest of the paragraph. Underline the topic sentences. Post the paragraphs. Then go get some of that yummy ice cream.

SUPER STARTER Give Alyssa a pen and a newspaper and ask her to find and underline five topic sentences. The two of you can read the corresponding paragraphs and have fun critiquing them.

Explain that some writers like to use rhetorical questions to start a paragraph. That means, instead of writing a regular topic sentence, the writers pose a question and then answer it themselves. For example, a paragraph might begin with, What's my favorite ice cream? and then go on in detail about what it is and why.

Next introduce Alyssa to some "fancy" sentence structures, those that make use of various phrases (groups of words). Here are several examples:

> Prepositional phrase: a preposition and its object. *For many people*, preparing a sandwich is easy.
>
> Infinitive phrase: *to* plus a verb. *To prepare a sandwich*, one needs a knife.
>
> Participial phrase: a verb form and modifiers. *Weakened by hunger*, my brother sat down.
>
> Gerund phrase: a verb ending in *-ing* that is used as a noun. *Making a big ham sandwich* is something I enjoy.)

Appositive phrase: a word or words placed after another word or words to identify it or them. My favorite snacks, *peanut butter and jelly sandwiches*, are also nutritious.

Ask Alyssa to write some topic sentences, using these kinds of phrases, and then complete the paragraphs, while you try to do the same. That means adding sentences with supporting details, illustrations, explanations, examples, or facts. Then vote for the best paragraphs and post the winners in the hallway.

Finally, assign Alyssa a report on her favorite book. The requirements are two or more paragraphs and a creative topic sentence, and she must proofread it. How? Sit down with Alyssa and help her check for good grammar, emphasize proper mechanics, check for spelling errors, and be careful with punctuation. Some hints on how to do that are in the next chapter. Meanwhile, please celebrate your kids' success. It is also your success.

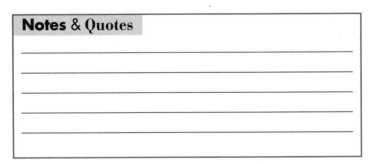

Notes & Quotes

Do you know the feeling of freedom that comes from learning a task so well you can then take liberties and branch out? Remember the first dish you ever cooked in your life, plain macaroni and cheese, and how nervous you were that it would turn out all right? But soon you advanced to other pasta. You learned to add bacon bits or ham chunks, then broccoli. In no time you were whipping up those crabmeat casseroles your neighbor raved over, the spinach lasagna your relatives requested, and your heavenly chicken and eggplant over noodles dish that still has your family clamoring for seconds and thirds.

Or maybe your first foray into food preparation came at the backyard barbecue. Oh, those first charbroiled hamburgers; half of them fell through the grill onto the hot coals. But later you became a master chef and learned to flip those patties with the best of them. All it took was practice, which led to refinements, which led to triumph.

Same with writing paragraphs. Once you master the ABC's, you just keep practicing. Soon you can write so well your ideas take flight and soar. Let's teach your kids how to do that next.

29 | Develop Your Own Writing Style

PARENT POINTER *Help your kids develop their own writing styles.*

Don't you have your own style in what you wear? Your hairstyle? How you decorate your home? Sure you do. You put your signature on everything you touch. Even at work, you handle required tasks according to your own system (or wish you could). Even in a huge corporation, or an immense bureaucracy, *your individuality*, your special approach to your work, makes all the difference. It's the real you, that contribution from within, that makes your work so satisfying.

That's the kind of feeling you want your kids to have. But in school a long list of rules prevails. Schools run by the book and tend to make our kids feel unimportant. Students, especially the more creative ones, can feel like they're in a straitjacket.

What better lifelong gift can you give them than a feeling of unlimited potential, a feeling of being valued, of having their best efforts recognized and encouraged? None! Yet how can you do that when schools are bound by bells, run by regulations, and geared to groups? All this routine can make individual students, your kids, feel powerless, left out, forgotten.

FYI

All you have to do is give your kids the power of the pen—or keyboard. With that they will always have a feeling of strength and freedom and know the fun of making choices, of being in charge of their learning.

Assume your task is to go 300 miles, from point A to point B, down a narrow dirt road, and you have only one mode of transportation: your feet. No way, you think.

But what if you had choices? You could ride in a taxi, drive a brand-new Lamborghini, or have a luxurious private jet standing by. Now getting from A to B isn't so bad. It might even be fun—just like your kids' trip to the next grade will be, from here on out.

Why? Because you're empowering them. You're giving them all the choices there are when confronted with one of the most frequent school tasks—writing assignments.

HELPFUL HOW-TO HINTS

SMART STARTER First buy Joanie a journal. Let her choose it herself, maybe one decorated with Dalmatians or one she can trim herself with stickers or colorful fabric. Get one for yourself too. Then ask Joanie to write something in her journal every day. Let her fill in the dates for the coming week, if she wants.

Tomorrow, after supper, get out your journals. Set the timer for five minutes and ask Joanie to write whatever she wants. You do the same. She may want to read to you what she's written. Maybe you want to read one of your sentences to her, maybe not.

After a week or two, ask Joanie to copy something from her journal onto a sheet of paper. Explain that journal writing is letting whatever thoughts we have emerge, just like letting everything grow that comes up in our yard. But now it's time to learn how to make a pretty garden: to pull the weeds and encourage the flowers. In writing that means checking over something we've written and working with it until it's the best it can be.

To do that, teach Joanie to proofread. That begins with reading what she's written very slowly. Out loud is best. Then post the following questions on a corkboard in her room (or in the den or kitchen), so she can ask herself:

1. Does it make sense?

2. Is every sentence a complete thought?

3. Was anything important left out?

Next comes making all the corrections Joanie wants to make. Encourage her to make as many changes as possible. This revision part is the *real* writing, the process during which she develops her own style, so put an asterisk next to every line she improves, every error she finds and corrects. Then post her best writing sample in a prominent place in the house. Adorn it with a flower border.

Finally, toss out a topic you know Joanie likes or one you both like. Then teach her to

> Brainstorm—jot down words or ideas that come to her
>
> Go over her list and circle key words
>
> Put those key words in order in a simple outline
>
> Decide on a topic sentence and write it out
>
> Write a rough draft, which will include appropriate details
>
> Read the rough draft out loud while asking herself the three posted questions
>
> Make all the corrections she can
>
> Do the final draft

Voilà! Joanie has done it. Aren't you both bursting with pride?

SUPER STARTER Jimmy is ready for a more advanced checklist, so type up this one to use when proofreading or revising.

Are the verbs correct and consistent?

Do all subjects and verbs agree?

Are the pronouns right?

Are all words spelled correctly?

Did I use the proper punctuation marks?

Ask Jimmy to write a book report. To get him started, type up this basic book-report start chart to fill out or keep it on file for him on the computer.

Title:

Author:

Main characters:

Conflict/problem:

Not long ago, I read a book about—

I selected this book because—

One of the most interesting characters in this book was—

The most exciting part in this book occurred when—

Other kids should/shouldn't read this book because—

If I had written this book, I would have added/excluded—

My final comments on this book are—

With these writing prompts at hand, Jimmy can then decide what was most remarkable about this book, make a quick outline—such as characters, conflict, lasting benefits— and write a first draft.

Of course, the next time Jimmy has a writing assignment, he can take more liberties, brainstorm, draw charts, make lists, and just let his pen flow. In other words, he can write to his heart's content. Should he ever run out of things to say, he can always go back to the book-report start chart.

What you're teaching Jimmy is to take control of his writing assignments. To make the process easier, have him write something every day. If he wants those expensive skates or that new video game, ask him to put it in writing. Remember, every time he writes something, he gains major scholastic strength. From that flows a feeling of esteem. In no time he'll get so fluent in his writing he'll devise his own proofreading system.

Soon Jimmy will print out his own writing checklist and come up with a series of shortcuts. Remind him that the computer spell checker works on a very basic level. It can't distinguish between words such as *too*, *to*, and *two*, for example. Therefore, computer spell checking is always only step one. The second step is human spell checking. Does Jimmy have a list of spelling demons posted? Does he know the difference between *accept* and *except*, for instance?

Finally, and most important, shower Jimmy with all the writing riches there are. Help him collect and post his favorite descriptive adjectives and strong verbs. Discuss with him over dinner not how he can improve his looks by cutting his long hair but how he can improve his writing by making his sentences short and to the point. (That's easy: Just chop off everything except your basic noun and verb.)

To lengthen a sentence he needs to know about conjunctions. There are:

> *coordinating* ones (and, but, or, for, nor)
>
> *subordinating* ones (although, as, as if, because, before, if, since, so that, than, till, until, unless, what, whenever, wherever, while, and so on)
>
> *correlative* ones (not only/but also; either/or; neither/nor; both/and; whether/or)

He should also know the usual sentence patterns:

1. Simple sentence, which has one subject and one verb (Yiyi wants to go camping.)

2. Compound sentence, which has two halves (clauses) each with a subject and a verb (Cameron couldn't make up her mind, and she would not take my advice.)

3. Complex sentence, which has one main sentence, or clause, and one dependent sentence, or clause (If you were to list your favorite TV shows, what would you include?)

4. Compound-complex, which has two main sentences, or clauses, and one dependent sentence, or clause (Before you call Seattle, you should check the number and you should also write it down.)

Once Jimmy can play around with sentence patterns, he can really develop his own composition style. So go for it. With your help Jimmy can become the emperor of English at his school. Be thrilled at his new skills. And then weave in the comment about getting that haircut.

Notes & Quotes

_____

_____

_____

_____

_____

Developing one's writing style and loving to write isn't just for school. It comes in handy throughout your kids' lifetime. Nor should learning be laborious. It should also contain laughter and lightheartedness. Let's make sure this happens. Let's lighten the load our kids have.

30 Write Letters, Notes, and Cards

PARENT POINTER *Teach your kids to write thank-you notes and letters and enjoy it.*

Do you enjoy sending birthday cards, or is that a chore for you, something you dread? Does the thought of getting out all those cards for major holidays send a shiver down your spine? Is compiling the annual family newsletter a pain?

It is for a lot of people. Yet even if you're among them, you do it. You know that letter writing is one of the oldest and most personal ways of communication, so it's something you respect—even while you moan about having to do it. Wouldn't it be nice if there was an easier method? Some way to take the sting out of snail-mailing things?

FYI

Luckily, now there is. All you have to do is enlist your kids' writing skills in the endeavor, and you're almost home free. By getting them involved in the family correspondence, you're not only saving yourself time, you're also enhancing their school skills.

Yes, when you teach your kids the joys of writing letters, memos, greeting cards, and thank-you notes, you're making them smarter scholastically and socially. You have to force your kids to write a thank-you note to Uncle Williston every year, you say? Fret no more. From now on, you're making it a fun brain game. Your kids won't be able to wait to join in.

HELPFUL HOW-TO HINTS

SMART STARTER Send Morrison on a treasure hunt in your home to find a nice box and have him decorate it with cutouts of his favorite cartoon characters or pictures of toys from a children's store catalog. Meantime, clear off some space for the special box in the den or family room, on a counter or desk or small table. That's going to be your correspondence corner from now on.

Collect family letters and notes that need answering in the box. Also have a calendar nearby, so whatever birthdays and other events are coming up can be clearly marked and noticed. Then help Morrison design his own greeting cards with the help of the family computer. All Morrison needs to do is collect his favorite sayings, jokes and riddles, daffy definitions, poems, sentences, or messages and copy them onto the cards.

In this way, Morrison creates individualized birthday, get-well, thank-you, New Year's, and all other types of card well in advance. He can keep whatever is needed in the correspondence line always in stock. He can also decorate the cards with photos, crayons, colored markers, or fun stamps. Soon his homemade cards will turn into real masterpieces.

Meanwhile, teach him to print address labels on the computer, or have him design his own labels or envelopes or stationery. He'll enjoy laying out a letterhead or drawing up party invitations. Then buy him some three-by-five note cards in various colors to decorate. He'll be proud to mail out another piece of Morrison mail; if the note goes to Grandma, you can add a few words, if you wish.

Long before any major holiday, Morrison will have cards and notes ready for the mailman. Of course, e-mail is another option, but be sure to explain to him that no hurtful gossip, dirty jokes, or mean stuff should ever be sent out, not even as a joke.

SUPER STARTER Have Monica write a letter to herself in which she tells of her daily events. Ask her to seal it and give it to you for safekeeping, not to be opened until she graduates from high school. She can also make a scrapbook out of the best letters she receives.

If Monica doesn't get any mail, you write to her. Once every week on Friday, write her a letter from work or e-mail her. In that letter, be sure to mention that you're expecting a letter back.

Mail for Monica will soon flood your box, if she uses letter writing as a tool to interview the oldest relatives in the family or someone still living in the small town where her parents grew up. When she studies World War II, have her write letters to veterans and interview them by mail. Or she can write to girls her age living on another continent. Perhaps her teacher or librarian can help her find the name of a middle school in New Delhi whose students will be thrilled to write back.

Best of all, Monica can take over the family complaint department. When a product you buy turns out to be shoddy, especially one that your kids use, have Monica write the manufacturer. Teach her the commonly used form of a business letter, which includes as a minimum

> the heading (Monica's address)
>
> the date (April 1, 2002)
>
> the salutation (Dear Mr. Toymaker)
>
> the body of the letter (one, two, or three polite paragraphs)

the closing (Sincerely)

the signature (Monica's full name)

This is a good time to remind her to brainstorm, make a quick outline (putting her most convincing points last), then write the rough draft and copy it over. And use her best handwriting. Handwritten letters often get more attention, especially if they're in Monica's best writing. She does know, doesn't she, that neatness counts? Always has and always will.

It's terrific for Monica to have a real reason for writing letters. Let her branch out: Send away for information, voice her opinion (to the local newspaper, congressmen, authors of books she reads), or offer congratulations to someone. And while Monica is turning into a fabulous correspondent, share the adventure. Write some letters together, with each one of you contributing a paragraph.

Finally, introduce Monica to some of the world's most famous letters. Find and read to her Thomas Jefferson's letter to his daughter Martha (written November 28, 1783), in which he tells her what to study. Or show her some of your old letters, the ones you've saved since you were a teenager. Then take her to the library and let her scout around for collections of letters that have literary merit and come up with her own list of best letter writers.

Notes & Quotes

_____

_____

_____

_____

You know, of course, that letters, notes, and cards, even silly ones, aren't just for today; they're timeless. So when you teach your kids to enjoy writing them, you're teaching them to turn their thoughts and feelings into small or big written monuments. How much joy do our letters bring? We don't know. But we do know that kids who correspond more learn more. And those who learn more leap ahead more—in schoolwork and in life.

Writing well and getting a kick out of it is something that will always stick with your kids. Whether they are applying to college, submitting scholarship applications, or filling out forms for high-level jobs, writing is crucial. Smart parents, and that includes you, constantly build on that skill. They know that the better their kids can express themselves, on paper or on the computer, the further they can go.

But that's not all your kids need to be able to do. Being able to express themselves orally is important as well.

Part VII: Verbal Smarts

Help your kids to . . .
know the English language well

After learning to write well, the next most crucial skill is being able to present information well orally. Speaking and explaining, giving presentations, or simply responding impressively aloud in class are all immensely valuable.

This is a very simple school tool to give your kids. Children are naturally intrigued by language. Just wait and see what will happen as you share with them the richness of our wonderful language in all its complexity and beauty.

TOP TIP
31 Enjoy Words

PARENT POINTER *Interest your kids in a wide variety of words.*

Are there any words you adore more than "I love you" and "The check's in the mail"? Maybe yes, maybe no. But if you're like most of us, you don't have time to worry about words. You simply *use* them, like change for the meter in the parking lot.

In truth, for the majority of people, words are just combinations of sounds they employ as the means to an end. They're satisfied with the roughly ten thousand words at their command and leave hundreds of thousands of other words unused.

In a way that's like having a huge forgotten account in a bank somewhere that nobody's getting to use. Why not tap into that resource? Why not give your kids the key to that hidden treasury?

FYI

We can look at words in various ways. We can study their histories, meanings, sounds, and structures. What matters most is that we enjoy them. According to Anatole France, "We think with words." The more words your kids know, the better they can think and the smarter they are.

HELPFUL HOW-TO HINTS

SMART STARTER Ask Nicole to name five favorite words and five words she's not that fond of. Draw pictures that represent those words with her. For example, by putting dots into the B of BUG and adding antennae, the letter can be made to look like an actual creepy crawler. Same goes for the S in SNAKE.

Ask her for a long word and help her subtract letters to make the word shorter. *School* becomes *cool*; *playground* can become *pay*, *lay*, *round*, or *pond*; and so on. Then ask Nicole to circle words in the newspaper that can be used similarly, and you do the letter subtractions while she watches.

Next, get Nicole to add letters to a short word. Start with *at*, which can grow to *rat*, *brat*, *berate*. Or *it*, which can turn into *its*, *sits*, *sites*, *spites*, *respites*, and more.

Then print a large N on a sheet of paper and ask her to list all the words she knows starting with that letter. Dictionaries are not allowed. The next day while driving her to school, call out the letter S and take turns with her naming as many S-words as you can.

Following that, give her the letter F and ask her for names of the following that begin with F: country or state, city, flower or plant, animal or bird, verb (past tense), first name, famous person (last name), and job. (Examples: France, Florence, fern, frog, flew, Fred, Ford [Henry], and fireman.) Then print up a chart with these or similar categories, pick another letter, and let her get to work. Nicole can use any reference materials she wants. When her friends come over, make a contest out of it by setting a time limit. Every correct answer is worth five points, and the winner gets to pick a prize.

Then ask Nicole to invent her own language. Have her look at a puppy and tell you what she would call a little dog if the words *puppy* and *dog* were not allowed. And what would she call a book, if she couldn't use that word? What about the sky? The stars? What would she call them? In no time Nicole will discuss various words and wonder out loud how we came up with them in the first place. And she'll giggle over words like *hubbub*, *razzle-dazzle*, and *tsetse fly*.

SUPER STARTER

Nick likes to collect things like sharks' teeth and arrowheads, so help him become a word collector. How many words can he name that end with *-city*? Does he know *sagacity, audacity, ferocity, authenticity*? Can he make those words into adjectives (*sagacious, audacious, ferocious, authentic*) and use them in sentences? What about words beginning with *cat*? (*catfish, catapult, catalog, catcher, catastrophe*) You'll both have fun when he starts getting into word activities like these if you take part in them.

Then ask Nick and his friends to go on a hunt for homonyms (words that sound alike but aren't spelled alike and don't mean the same thing) and collect as many pairs as possible (*carat, carrot; isle, aisle; four, fore*).

Play "unfamiliar words" with Nick. You give him a word you know he doesn't know and let him guess the definition before he looks up the correct one. Then let him scout for an obscure word you've never heard of, and you guess what it means and look that one up. Post all new words the two of you learn and use them every so often.

Practice reading difficult texts with Nick, just a paragraph at a time. Pretend you're both Roman orators and have to speak to crowds without benefit of a microphone. Later read Oliver Wendell Holmes's "Old Ironsides" aloud together—as a chorus of two—and let the sounds of our splendid language embrace and bond you both (Nick's school librarian will help you locate the poem). Then ask Nick to find two synonyms in the first stanza (*ensign, banner*) and from then on each day have him give you a synonym for words like *car* (*vehicle, automobile, taxi*) or *spit* (*sputum, spittle, phlegm*). I guarantee you that sooner or later he'll burst out laughing; you too.

Finally, teach Nick phrases from foreign languages:

> ad infinitum: without end
>
> bona fide: genuine

crème de la crème: the best of the best

en masse: in a large body

esprit de corps: group spirit

je ne sais quoi: I don't know what, something undefinable

che serà serà: what will be will be

quid pro quo: something given for something else

Also teach Nick some basic acronyms or abbreviations, such as

anon: anonymous

Btu: British thermal unit

CEO: chief executive officer

CPA: certified public accountant

EU: European Union

IRA: individual retirement account

NAACP: National Association for the Advancement of Colored People

OPEC: Organization of Petroleum Exporting Countries

RSVP: répondez s'il vous plaît (please reply)

ZIP: zone improvement plan

And from now on, have Nick scour the newspaper and find some foreign phrases and acronyms to stump *you*. It tickles kids to know more than their parents. Let them feel that elation, and feel the joy they get when they make new discoveries.

Notes & Quotes

_____

_____

_____

_____

_____

There are so many word-related discoveries just waiting for your kids. After all, this is the third millennium, and through the Internet they are connected to the whole world. Why not expand their global vocabulary? Besides making your kids smarter, you'll contribute to their feeling of kinship with kids of other nations.

For your kids to be in charge of their immense verbal empire, they have to explore the structural makeup of words. This in turn will make them commanders and directors of their vocabulary.

32 Become a Word Master

PARENT POINTER *Teach your kids to manipulate and master words.*

When you eat a slice of delicious cake, do you use your sense of taste to decide if lemon, almonds, vanilla, chocolate, caramel, ginger, or hazelnut were used in whipping it up? I do. And when I see the outside of a home I like, I immediately wonder about its layout. How are the rooms arranged? How functional or creative is its blueprint?

While cakes and cottages can come in many flavors and designs, the same is not true for words. Words have a very simple structure. And once your kids know that structure, they won't feel cowed by new words ever again.

FYI

Basically, words consist of only three parts: roots, prefixes, and suffixes. Prefixes are letters put before a word to change its meaning (*dis-* as in *disbelieve*). Suffixes are letters attached to the end of a word to form a new word (*-ness* in *happiness*).

By learning just a few prefixes and suffixes, kids can discover a large number of new words and put them to use. Here are just a few examples. Prefixes are in the first column, suffixes in the second.

com- (with): compose	-able (capable of being): usable
de- (down): decline	-er (one who does): teacher
ex- (out of): exclude	-ful (full of): spoonful
im- (in, into): immigrant	-ish (like, tending toward): roundish
re- (again, back): return	-less (without): painless

HELPFUL HOW-TO HINTS

SMART STARTER Ask Brad to print the listed prefixes and suffixes on flash cards and have him find words in the newspaper that contain these parts. Can he underline the prefixes or suffixes in the following words and guess what they might mean?

comprehend

negotiable

recitation

photographer

Next, ask him to try to form new words himself by using those same word parts.

On another occasion, ask Brad to use these common roots:

pend (meaning hang)

vers, vert (meaning turn)

vid (meaning see)

How many words can he form with these roots? Help him come up with more.

Explain to Brad that suffixes that begin with a vowel can cause a spelling change. For example, love + ing = loving.

Also, when the suffix -*est* is added to a word ending in *y*, the *y* becomes *i*, as in happy + est = happiest.

Meanwhile, some words double their last letter when the suffix -*ing* is added: stop + ing = stopping.

With this in mind, send Brad to scout around. Can he find similar examples in the newspaper or in a book he's reading, copy them, and bring them to you?

Also mention that quite a few of our words are:

> borrowed from other languages: toboggan from Native Americans
>
> compounds (words put together): lunchroom
>
> shortened: dorm from dormitory
>
> named after places: hamburger (from Hamburg in Germany)

Then ask Brad to copy twenty five- or six- (or more) letter words from a magazine, and together you two will look at their structure to figure out where the words may be from and what they mean.

SUPER STARTER When Bethany wants to know more about the world of words, tell her that some suffixes indicate nouns (-*ance*, -*ity*, -*ment*, -*ness*). Others form verbs (-*ate*, -*ize*, -*fy*), and still others adjectives (-*y*, -*al*, -*ible*, -*ive*). Knowing this, she can recognize what part of speech a new word is before she knows what it means.

Then put her to work. Can she think of a word for each of the different suffixes just mentioned? Have her try, first without a dictionary, then with one. Or, better, you two work on the assignment together.

Then it's Bethany's turn, all by herself. Can she tell what part of speech the following words are just by looking at the suffixes?

> tangential (adjective)
>
> cauterize (verb)
>
> infeasibility (noun)

Then it's time for her to look up these three words, find the definitions, and write sentences with them. Next time she talks to her grandmother, ask her to use one of these words. Won't Nana be surprised? And while she's talking to her grandmother, tell Bethany to ask Nana for a list of ten unusual words for Bethany to take apart, analyze, manipulate, master, and post on the fridge.

Then have Bethany copy down this sentence—The *griber-itxky bloophrerl* will *anigstwisn* quickly—and tell you what it means. She won't know, of course; no one does. The italicized words are nonsense, but their positions can tell Bethany immediately what part of speech they are. The first italicized word is an adjective; the second word is a noun; and the third is a verb. Now give Bethany the most difficult text you have, have her copy two sentences she doesn't understand, then sit down with her and see if she can't figure out what parts of speech the unknown words are. Remind her that if she finds *the* or *a* in front of a word, it's probably a noun or an adjective preceding a noun.

Finally, tell Bethany that all the words in the world are hers, so she should be daring with them, not shy. Use those big words, if not every day, then at least once in a while. Get to know them well. She should consider herself a conductor leading an orchestra, and all the words are her instruments. Some are plain and scratch out a simple tune, but others sing the most melodious songs. Then ask her, What's the longest word in the world?

The answer is SMILES: there's a MILE between its first and last letters!

Notes & Quotes

_____

_____

_____

_____

_____

We've only just scratched the surface of the wonders of words so far. There's much more for your kids to learn. Let's teach them the two secret languages of English. Those two secret languages are Greek and Latin.

While the English we speak today comes from a prehistoric language called Indo-European, a large number of words from other languages, especially from Greek and Latin, were mixed in over the centuries. Knowing a lot of those Greek and Latin words can help your kids tremendously.

33 | Learn Latin and Greek Roots, Prefixes, and Suffixes

PARENT POINTER *Teach your kids the Latin and Greek roots, prefixes, and suffixes.*

Most of our jobs and professions have their own technical terms, also known as jargon. That comes from the specialized field we spend our working hours in. For example, in television, we have the expression *prime time*, the hours when the largest audience or maximum viewership is available.

The years your kids spend in school, especially those from kindergarten through eighth grade, are scholastic prime time for them. Maximum learning can take place in those years, before they're faced with all the challenges teenagers encounter today.

FYI

You can maximize your kids' learning years by teaching them the inside jargon of schoolwork, textbooks, and standardized tests. That's done by making them familiar with the most common Greek and Latin word parts, each of which can automatically introduce them to five, ten, fifteen, twenty, twenty-five, or even fifty brand-new words.

How do you start?

HELPFUL HOW-TO HINTS

SMART STARTER Ask Paige to name several foreign languages. Then tell her that many are related because, thousands of years ago, they came from the same source. That's why quite a few words are similar, no matter what language we're speaking. For example:

English: mother

Spanish: *madre*

French: *mere*

Dutch: *moeder*

German: *mutter*

Tell Paige to choose any word she likes and then ask you or a friend, neighbor, teacher, or librarian to help her translate this word into several foreign languages and see if there is any relationship between the translations.

Next explain to Paige that English contains bits and pieces from many other languages, but since no one has time to study them all, it's best to concentrate on the two that crop up most frequently in the more difficult English words: Greek and Latin. Can Paige locate on the map some of the countries where these languages (or their modern cousins) are spoken, such as Greece, Italy, and Spain? Can she draw those countries?

Then teach Paige to count to three in Latin—*uno* (uni) *duo*, *tre* (tri)—and show her how many words she can now understand.

Say: So what do you think the words *uniform* (of one form), *duplex* (two units), and *tricycle* (three wheels) really mean? Can you think of more words using these Latin roots?

Finally, present her with these Greek roots:

auto: self

bio: life

chron: time

graph, *gram*: write

logos: word, thought

Then the two of you can get to work and name or track down as many words as possible with those Greek roots in them. Who can find more?

SUPER STARTER Paolo needs a more advanced list of Latin or Greek roots to get him started on his vocabulary quest, so buy him two file boxes and 500 index cards and give him the following roots:

LATIN	GREEK
capt: take	*logy*: study of
cred: believe	*phil*: loving
dic, *dict*: say	*phon*: sound
fac, *fec*: make	*soph*: wise
port: send or carry	*pseudo*: false
scrit, *script*: write	*tele*: far
spec: see	
voc, *vok*: speak	

Ask Paolo, Can you come up with one or more words for each root? Can you find more words with these roots in the dictionary? Then say, Write those words on the index cards, with the definitions on the back. Label one file box FAMILY, the other PAOLO. All done.

Another day, ask Paolo to write a sentence using each new word on the back of the cards (under the definition). Meanwhile, keep adding more interesting words to the cards, even if they're unrelated to Greek or Latin. All words are records of human development over the centuries, and you want to make sure your kids are fascinated by them.

One evening before bedtime, play a game with Paolo. Hold up the cards so he can see the words, and ask him what they mean. If he knows them and can use them in a sentence, the cards go into the file box with his name on it. If he's unsure, put the card back into the FAMILY box and, when he's not looking, sneak in some tough new vocabulary cards of your own.

Ask Paolo's teacher for a vocabulary-builder series she recommends or buy a vocabulary workbook in a bookstore. Then announce a "root for the day" by posting a Latin or Greek root on the fridge and declare that person the winner who can name the most unusual word including the root (or the longest, shortest, or most complex). You can involve not only your family but Paolo's friends and their parents in the vocabulary drills.

In his hunt for more difficult words, Paolo is sure to come across some paragraphs with words that don't have any of the obvious roots in them. That's when context clues will help him out. *Context* refers to the sentences in which the strange word appears.

Let's arm Paolo with three types of context clues:

1. Definition clues: Euphony is a pleasant-sounding tone. (Here the writer defines the word for us.)

2. Synonym or antonym clues: I don't like their constant dissembling and lying. (In this case, *lying* is a synonym for *dissembling*). Or: She never dissembled; she was always totally honest. (In that case, *was honest* is the antonym of *dissembled*.)

3. Comparison or contrast clues: The climb up the hill was arduous, unlike the easy stroll I expected.

On the next car trip, call out *ject* (throw), for example, and let everyone in the car pepper you orally with *eject, reject, inject, deject, project, object, subject, conjecture, projectile, objective, subjectivity, abject,* and other *ject* words. Then go on to *claud, clud, clus* (to close) and start over. What fun—and what interesting new words your kids will learn. They may even invent their own and catch you when you're trying to sneak a word past them that doesn't even exist. You're out, Mom, Dad, out of the game. 'Bye!

Notes & Quotes

_____

_____

_____

_____

_____

Whenever your kids impress someone in school or down the road with their increased vocabulary and smarts, you'll be there with them. And while memorizing Greek and Latin roots can be arduous at times, your kids will have nothing but fun with the next top teacher tip.

34 Study the Dictionary and the Thesaurus

PARENT POINTER *Encourage your kids to study the dictionary and the thesaurus.*

These days teachers often complain about their students' *paucity*. But it's not that the children lack money; they don't have enough words at their command. That's one reason why cursing is now so pervasive among kids. Instead of varying the way they express themselves, kids just latch on to a few four-letter words and use them over and over, in their conversations and in their writing. This can make their talking offensive and their writing, *like, bor-ing*. Offensive language gets them in trouble and dull writing reaps less than stellar grades.

To overcome that problem, all you have to do is make your kids instantly rich—in vocabulary.

FYI

A dictionary is a treasury of words. A thesaurus is a menu of words grouped by meanings. Both are incredible fountains of learning. And they are cheap.

You probably have one or both at your house; if not, buy them. There are special junior dictionaries for various ages. Then give them a place of honor, the middle of the dining room table or the coffee table in the den. There will be no more boring talk at your house. And the cursing will get better too, or at least become more creative. Isn't it an improvement for one kid to call the other an unsagacious ignoramus instead of a stupid idiot?

HELPFUL HOW-TO HINTS

SMART STARTER Play "dictionary" with Reece. Open the dictionary to any page, choose an appropriate word, and ask Reece what it means. Then he does the same and puts *you* on the spot. Add all unknown words to a master list (or the file boxes mentioned in the last chapter).

Ask Reece to skim the dictionary for a word with fifteen or more letters (like quintessentially). Next you'll have to find one with sixteen letters.

Have a five-word spelling bee with Reece every evening between his spaghetti and his Jell-O. Ask him to look up *spaghetti* in the dictionary to see if it has another meaning (it does, in the field of electricity).

Next time you make a sandwich for Reece, say, Do you know where the word *sandwich* comes from? If he doesn't, tell him to look it up. (John Montagu, 1718-1792, Fourth Earl of Sandwich, never wanted to stop gambling long enough to eat a sit-down dinner, so the sandwich was invented for him.) Is there anything Reece likes to keep doing? Ask him to think of a new word or phrase that should be invented for him, and to invent one for you. Watch out!

Next ask Reece to write a new definition for his favorite word. Tell him to include what dictionary entries include:

pronunciation

other forms (listed under *weather* are *weathered, weathering, weathers*)

part of speech

usage: whether the word is slang, dialect (regional), or archaic (very old)

synonyms (other words with the same meaning)

idioms (phrases with a different meaning, e.g., *under the weather* means *not feeling well*)

Also introduce Reece to a thesaurus, and the next time he whines, ask if he could please grumble, whimper, complain, yowl, howl, wail, mutter, snivel, or yammer instead. That will not only make Reece stop whining but give you a chance to show him how he can find a better word for the same overused words he has been using. Tell him to investigate some alternatives for the word "stuff." Then appoint him as word cop for one week. His job: to catch you every time you use a trite word or phrase. Reward him with a quarter each time he does.

SUPER STARTER Ask Rory to write down two favorite words, then introduce her to the magnificent *Oxford English Dictionary* (*OED*), which may be found in her school or town library. In this dictionary the history of words is detailed. The date the words were used first is mentioned and whatever changes the words went through are explained. Rory will be fascinated by all the information she'll find—and so will you.

Next time Rory's eating a s'more, tell her about a vegetarian (1794–1851) who wanted to reform the diet of Americans and advocated whole wheat flour, coarsely ground. Can she find out his name (Sylvester Graham) and write a dictionary entry for a new word that she will coin? Then tell her to jump two centuries ahead mentally and write down how the word might have changed.

When Rory has time, ask her to look up several first names in the dictionary and tell you what they meant originally or what language they came from. She'll find out that her middle name, Anna, came from Hannah and means graciousness in Hebrew. Can she come up with a fabulous meaning for Rory?

Ask Rory to become your teacher and give you a new useful word every day for a week. First she has to research the word, show how it will be helpful to you in some way, write a sentence using it, and teach you an antonym (opposite) of it. On Saturday, she'll test you on all your new words; if you miss one, you have to help her with her chores. Serves you right.

Next time Rory talks about her green sweatshirt, ask her to name all the "greens" she can. Then have her look up the word in the thesaurus and copy her favorite synonyms for green on a note card. When your next birthday comes, ask Rory to write you a short story, using such glamorous green colors as chartreuse, emerald, jade, and aquamarine as the names of her characters. And then at the end of Rory's story, suggest that little plain old *green* might emerge as the hero because nature gave it such prominence.

Ask Rory what her favorite foreign language is, have her give you a reason, then buy her a dictionary in that language. And every so often, say: I wonder what the word *cookie* is in French or Spanish. Can you look it up? Then make it a point to learn a few foreign words with her. Rory is learning much more than new words. She's breaking down barriers, expanding her mind, adding to her store of knowledge. Her pride in her achievements will soar, and she'll be far too busy studying and thinking to get involved in age-inappropriate or plain wrong behaviors.

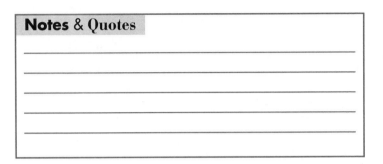

Notes & Quotes

The bottom line: Spending just a few minutes here and there with a dictionary and a thesaurus will really make your kids smarter, brighter, and more resourceful. In short, you enable them to live the best lives possible. So forge ahead, this time on to some real fun activities.

35 Play Word Games

PARENT POINTER *Teach your kids to enjoy word games and puzzles.*

Some people claim the brain is a muscle and, like the other muscles of our body, needs a regular tough workout. But nothing but tough workouts can be discouraging. Make sure your kids get some brain exercises that are fun too. You do that by getting everyone in the family involved, by adding a touch of healthy competition to the activities—and by having a small prize attached. That does wonders.

FYI

Healthy competitions plus a small reward or prize don't only bring smiles and laughter to a family, they also makes playtime more interesting for your kids and their friends. When your children's classmates come for a birthday party, instead of having them play softball, have them play word-search games. All it takes is a smidgen of creativity to get them started.

HELPFUL HOW-TO HINTS

SMART STARTER Try each of the following games with Tessa and then let her pick the ones she likes best for the times her friends or cousins come over. Or she can play via e-mail with her granddad.

First play "Almost Twins." You choose an adjective and a noun and Tessa has to respond with a similar pair. You say "cute dog." She answers with "pretty hound" or "attractive canine" or "charming mutt." (If there are questions or challenges, the thesaurus rules. Only words listed under *dog* and *cute* can be used.)

Next comes "Chain Reaction." You begin with a compound word and Tessa will try to name another compound word that begins with the last part of the word you name. Then it's your turn to name a compound word that starts with the last part of Tessa's word.

For example:

You: councilman. Tessa: manhour. You: hourglass. Tessa: glassware. You: warehouse. Tessa: housemaster. You: mastermind. And so on.

After that it's time for "Adverb Adventure." Call out this sentence to Tessa: Venus played tennis _____. Then ask her to fill in the blank with an adverb (such as *nicely*, *skillfully*, *brilliantly*, *capably*, *smartly*, *easily*). Next, Tessa will test your knowledge of adverbs with this sentence: My mom laughs _____ *or* My dad cooks _____ on the grill.

Explain how to play "Add One On" to Tessa. One player starts with a two-letter word, the next adds a letter to make it three letters, the next makes it four, and so on. Thus, *or* can becomes *our*, then *four*, then *flour*, then *flours*; *it* becomes *wit*, then *writ*, then *write*, then *writer*.

Ask Tessa what her favorite vowel is. If she says A, call out five words that need an A to grow (for example, fir → fair; men → mean; den → dean; try → tray; ply → play).

Using an educational Web site, print out several word-search puzzles for Tessa or construct your own. Even better, have Tessa look through the newspaper, find ten interesting words, print them into a blank grid either horizontally, vertically, forward, or backward, and then fill up the rest of the blank squares with letters picked at random. You'll need ten clues—one for each word (number 1 means . . . , number 2 means . . . , number 3 means . . .). And then *you* get to work, trying to find the words Tessa hid. Good luck.

SUPER STARTER

Challenge Tennyson, who already likes playing Scrabble and Password, with the word activity called "Yes or No." Ask him:

Can a bird be an *egress*? (No, it means exit.)

Is it impossible to make a *lapidarian* sandwich? (Yes, it means cut in stone.)

Can anybody tame an *eryngo* and teach it some tricks? (No, it's a plant.)

Then it's Tennyson's turn to try to trick you with three yes-no questions of his own. Watch out.

Next, scramble something for him—not eggs but a few fine words, such as:

stsasi = a_____ (assist)

lsesslef = s_____ (selfless)

eeerpcratu = r_____ (recuperate)

Then ask Tennyson to create a word scramble for words beginning with each letter of the alphabet. Have him type and print out his own ABC scramble for other kids in the neighborhood. And while he's working on the ABC scramble, ask him to include some of his own fun phrases, like

> your nose
>
> right
>
> (That translates to "*right* under *your nose*.")

Keep on developing Tennyson's inquisitive attitude toward words by having him help you do the crossword puzzle in the newspaper each day. Or maybe he can start the puzzle by himself, and you help him later with the missing words.

Another day, ask him to use the letters in his name to describe himself.

> Terrific
>
> Energetic
>
> Nature-oriented
>
> Nosy (sometimes)
>
> Young
>
> Smart
>
> Outgoing
>
> Noble (trying to be)

Then create a name "poem" for a relative whose birthday is coming up.

The next time play "Find-All-Five" with Tennyson. Ask him to search through the dictionary for words containing all five vowels, such as *cauliflower* or *equation*. Or come up with other stipulations, such as: Can you find a word with three *m*'s, four *e*'s or five *n*'s? (Immemorial, everywhere, nonconventional.)

Finally, here comes the most fun: Can Tennyson track down all the words in town that are misspelled? Same goes for the newspaper. Or the product labels of cereals. Can he listen to TV announcers and catch errors they make? And then can he write a letter pointing out the errors to the appropriate sources, but in an affable, agreeable, amiable, and congenial manner? Can he persuade his school newspaper to publish some of his word puzzle creations? Have his teacher share them with other classes? Can he share some of the fun he's getting out of word games with the rest of his world? Go, Tennyson.

Notes & Quotes

_____

_____

_____

_____

_____

Once your kids get used to enjoying brain games, all kinds of fascinating words will be forever at their command. Whole word clusters and families will be their friends. Bonding with their language will empower your kids as they climb the scholastic ladder. And that same can-do attitude will help them as they face whatever hurdles they encounter along the way.

Part VIII: Testing Smarts

Help your kids to . . .
learn the best ways to take tests

Knowing how to take tests is vitally important, for all schools have checkpoints in place, inspection times when what your kids have learned will be assessed. There's really no way kids can escape getting rated on their scholastic prowess.

It's like running a race. The runner with the best shoes, who has trained the most and is the best prepared and equipped physically and mentally, will probably end up in first place. Same with students. It's not enough just to imbue them with knowledge; you should also instruct them on how to give evidence of that knowledge, in whatever format they may be requested to do so.

TOP TIP
36 | Know the Test Types

PARENT POINTER *Teach your kids about the different kinds of tests.*

Winston Churchill said the trick to managing a substance or force is not to let it manage you but to learn to manage it.

That's the case with tests. Unfortunately, many people are afraid of tests and, even in adulthood, still wake up from nightmares and relive the horrible pressure they felt as kids when faced with a major exam. The reason for this is that, as children, they were mastered by their tests and never learned to master them. But that doesn't have to happen.

FYI

Kids today can learn to have no fear of any test. And, as with anything tough or new that we try to do, once the fear is gone, the task is half done.

Teachers report that some of the most precious moments in the classroom occur when they give a quiz and every child in the room is prepared. How eagerly the students reach for the quiz, glance at it, read the questions, and, bending over the desk, fill in all the information. On occasions like these, a special ambiance settles over the class. There's no noise, except for the rustling of sheets and the sound of pencils gliding over paper. Here or there, a little tongue may dart across a lip to urge the sharpened pencil on. Now and then, when the children look up, their eyes shine brightly. And they smile, all of them; they know their material and they're so proud.

Equip your kids with the tools that will help them sail right through their tests in school. Make sure they also experience the wonderful feeling of *I know!*

HELPFUL HOW-TO HINTS

SMART STARTER Talk to McGuire about the kinds of tests you've taken in the past, the reasons behind them, and the fact that they can be fun. Yes, fun. Next, ask him to toss a ball of scrap paper into the trash can. If he doesn't make it the first time, let him try again. He may want to move closer or stand over the can until he hits his mark. Then tell him, It's the same with every test in the world. Practicing and figuring out the best angles, the best methods, will make any test a snap.

Later, ask McGuire to call out a list of rewards for you to write down. He may include: going skating, seeing a movie with friends, horseback riding, camping with you, getting the latest video game. After that, help him choose the one activity or purchase that's uppermost on his mind—and that's doable, given your family circumstances—and circle it.

As we know, success breeds success. Tell McGuire that this reward is attached to an improved grade in his worst subject, or his next-to-worst one. Discuss what that is, then set a daily study time aside for this subject. Make sure McGuire has a study place and knows what to study; then see that his surroundings are conducive to studying.

Next, find out what kind of test the teacher gives in this subject. Is it a spelling test? If so, divide up the list of words and call out a mini spelling test every day.

If the test is teacher-made, go over the chapter review in the book with McGuire. The next evening, design a practice test for him that's probably similar to the one he'll have. The following week, choose some key sentences from the chapter and have him fill in the blanks. Another time, prepare ten true-false questions on the material.

Also inform McGuire's teacher of the new plan and ask for help, including practice tests from previous years or old workbooks, worksheets, and study guides. Then have a quiz session every night—only three questions—and another one every morning.

For variety, write out some multiple-choice questions on the topic for McGuire, or have him write them out and test *you*. In short, by the time the actual test comes around, McGuire will know the material like the back of his hand. His score will improve; you can count on that. Post the higher grade and pick a date for the camp-out.

SUPER STARTER In Marnie's case, start with her teacher. Ask him, Why do you think Marnie's grades are low? Then find out where the problem lies.

PROBLEMS	SOLUTIONS
Studying	Double her study time
Classroom work	Ask for Marnie to be moved up front
Notebook	Help her organize or improve it
Reading	Double her reading time
Concentration	Teach her to concentrate better
Tests	Give her practice tests of all kinds (see Smart Starter)

Ask Marnie to design a record sheet of school tests for herself, such as the one below, so she can monitor her progress, and for every improvement she makes, compliment and reward her.

Test (Chapter 1): Date_____ Score_____
                  Problem_____ Solution_____
Test (Chapter 2): Date_____ Score_____
                  Problem_____ Solution_____

Let Marnie predict her next test scores. As she begins to see how handsomely extra studying, reading, and taking practice tests pay off, have her set a date for bringing up her grades and then try to beat that date. Ask her to tell you what you can do to help her improve her scores.

Visit a commercial learning center, check out their testing tools, and go home and download similar test-preparation helpers from the Internet. Print out some fun worksheets related to Marnie's lesson and supervise her while she does them.

If Marnie still doesn't get the test grades she's hoping for, teach her to manage her time better. First observe her while she studies for twenty minutes. Write down how often she gets up, yawns, gets something to drink, gazes off into the distance. Then tell her that from now on any time she catches herself not studying, she'll have to add a minute to her study time. But if she can keep concentrating without interruption for twenty minutes, she'll get a break or some juice or water.

Also, print out several "top test quest" sheets for Marnie and have her fill in the following blanks:

> When? (date of test) _____
>
> What? (which chapters will be covered)
>
> _____
>
> Review dates? (when the material was reviewed)
>
> _____
>
> Practice tests? (which ones and how many taken)
>
> _____
>
> Old quizzes and homework gone over? (when)
>
> _____
>
> Weak spots? (list them) _____

Then ask Marnie a few questions on her test prep system and help her examine it for any problem areas.

Celebrate every top test grade with Marnie. Bake a special cake for her A in social studies. Make a banner to honor her for that top score on her science quiz. Post all outstanding spelling tests. Remember: Success breeds success!

Make friends with the parents of kids who score high on tests and glean some tips from them. Maybe your kids can strike up a friendship and start studying together. Getting ready for an exam is extra fun when done with a friend.

Please also teach Marnie not to be upset over a low test score. On the contrary, tell her it gives her a chance to investigate her method of getting ready for the next test. Be sure to stress that there's no school test that can't be made up, taken over, or learned from.

Notes & Quotes

_____

_____

_____

_____

_____

Sometimes a low grade is needed to wake students up. It helps to motivate them and pulls parents and kids closer. So always, while working for high test scores, tell your kids that what they learn is most important, what knowledge they will take with them to the next grade and beyond.

Say, A low score is just part of the learning process, OK? Not to be ignored, just used as a stimulus to do better. Strive and thrive.

Just as there are basic test types, so are there basic test-taking techniques. They come in handy, especially when your kids have to take end-of-the-year or standardized tests, which many states now give. They are called *standardized* because they are presented to all kids with exactly the same directions and within the same time frame. In many cases those tests determine whether students are admitted to advanced classes—or even move to the next grade.

37 Learn Test-taking Techniques

PARENT POINTER *Teach your kids the best test-taking techniques.*

Most standardized tests are multiple-choice and lengthy. Naturally, all schools want their students to perform well on them because the school system's reputation may depend on the results.

FYI

As a parent or caregiver, you want the school to have a good academic reputation, but even more important is your children's ability to achieve. For that reason, you need to do whatever you can do to help them through their tests, whether they loom weekly, monthly, at the end of a semester, or at the end of the school year.

Fortunately, according to top teachers, there are only five basic techniques and five advanced ones, and they can help in every test situation. Once your kids know them, they're all set.

HELPFUL HOW-TO HINTS

SMART STARTER First, make Vida familiar with the test surroundings. Ask her teacher whether Vida's class will take any test outside her regular classroom. If so, be sure to take Vida to that room a week in advance and let her walk around and get used to it.

Second, tell Vida to listen to or read the test directions slowly and to underline important statements. Unless she's told otherwise, she can mark the test booklet up, circle words, or put check marks on them. Ask her teacher for several practice tests from previous years, read the directions to Vida, and show her what's important and what's not.

Third, explain to Vida that she should scan the whole test first before she begins. It's good to know what's ahead of her. Not knowing how many parts there are can be scary. Give her a practice booklet and show her how to scan it.

Fourth, tell Vida that it's best to take her time as she works through the test. It's not a race; she won't be graded on finishing first. She should read each question slowly, think it over, and then answer. Work with her on that skill.

Fifth, Vida needs to know that if she comes across a difficult section, she should skip it and return to it later. It doesn't make sense to spend a long time puzzling over one or two questions and then have time run out before getting to what she knows. Much better to return to the difficult problems later. Practice with Vida on skipping the tough questions and then going back to them.

SUPER STARTER

First, show Van how to budget his time, using either his own watch or the schoolroom clock. Practice with an old test or one you concoct. Also tell him to determine which sections count most heavily and spend the most time on them.

Second, tell Van to write down all the major dates, key words, important rules, and notable names he has memorized in the margin of the test as soon as he is handed a copy. That way he can clear his mind and concentrate only on the questions at hand.

Third, if Van is taking a math test, tell him to write neatly, show every step of his solution, and work each problem in more than one way if possible, so he'll catch any errors.

Fourth, to answer multiple-choice questions efficiently, Van should quickly eliminate the two answers that are obviously wrong and then attack the two that remain. One of them has to be the right one.

Finally—and this is very important—if Van has time left at the end of the testing period, he should go over all his answers again. A good way is to cover his earlier answers with a sheet of paper and pretend he's starting from scratch. Explain to Van that we all make careless mistakes, and he should do his best to find them himself. He should just make believe he's a spelling, math, and fact checker, and this test is someone else's work.

When the test results come back, it's best to make a copy of what was missed. What is there that Van doesn't understand? Where are his learning gaps? Have him make a list of what specific questions he didn't get right and find out from his teachers how these gaps can be filled. Also ask Van for his impression of the test and make a note of his comments. And, of course, really praise him for taking his schoolwork and his tests seriously.

Notes & Quotes

_____

_____

_____

In the time between now and the next big test, spring into action.

Divide whatever big gaps your kids have in their school skills into little ones and fill them with learning. Keep telling your kids how great taking a test can be when they know all the answers.

Give them little quizzes, only a question or two per day, that are especially designed by you to strengthen any scholastic weaknesses your kids have.

If you have to, take time off from work and have the standardized test results explained to you by the guidance counselor. Be glad you discovered your kids' lack of progress early enough to attack the problem. Give it your best efforts. And with each special drill you pick to help them move ahead, you'll be giving your kids hope, courage, confidence, and a big part of your heart.

Whenever you can, practice with your kids. Include in this practice another important test-taking skill: answering essay questions.

38 Practice for Essay Tests

PARENT POINTER *Teach your kids how to practice for essay tests.*

While the tests your kids face in school can come in a multitude of designs, there are only two main types: (1) The objective test, which has many questions, perhaps twenty to over a hundred, and requires short fast answers; and (2) the essay type, much tougher for most kids, which may have only four or five questions, each of which counts much more than one of many objective test questions and involves writing skills.

Most teachers prefer a combination of these two types. They want kids who race through the matching, true/false, multiple-choice, or fill-in-the-blank sections to slow down and spend time on the essay part. Also, they want to test for deeper understanding of the particular topic, and essay tests help do that.

FYI

It's important for your kids to know what kinds of tests their teachers are giving. Once they know that, your kids can get prepared. How will they know? Just have them ask the teacher during the review class, "How many essay questions will be on the test tomorrow?" The rest is easy.

HELPFUL HOW-TO HINTS

SMART STARTER Writing develops from talking, so from early on have Walker talk about an event or a picture at length. Prod him to go on by asking, And then what happened? or, What else do you notice?

Similarly, once Walker knows an essay test is coming up, help him to pick key topics from the history chapter the test will cover. Let him tell you all he knows about them. Prod him to name more and more facts about the life of the president he's been studying, for example.

Next, give Walker a blank sheet and have him write down all the facts he can remember about the president and then group them.

> Birth and death dates, early life, education
>
> Contribution to society, major breakthroughs, programs
>
> Final legacy (what he is remembered for today)

Then give this sample topic to Walker: "The Importance of John Adams." Ask him to come up with a topic sentence, list the details, make a brief outline, and write the essay in his best handwriting.

Before handing the essay to you, Walker needs to proofread it by checking his punctuation (Does every sentence have an end mark?), capitalization (Are all proper nouns capitalized?), and spelling (Is *diplomat* spelled correctly?).

Read the essay with Walker, put stars in the margin next to his good sentences, and post the essay in a place of honor in your home.

SUPER STARTER Tell Willow to read all the essay questions before she begins. Sometimes she'll be given a choice, such as, *Answer three of the following questions.* By reading all of them carefully, she can concentrate on the ones she feels most comfortable with.

Ask Willow to practice by anticipating the essay questions her teacher will give her. Ask her to write them down, outline the major points, and jot down dates, places, and important events or quotes that will support her outline. In other words, tell Willow to prepare a skeleton essay for every question she thinks may be on the test.

Next, have Willow choose the one question most likely to crop up and flesh out her skeleton essay by writing it out completely. Teach her to time herself. If there's enough time, she should copy the essay over, after making as many changes as she can. If there isn't enough time, she should just proofread it as carefully as possible.

Read the following topic sentence from one of Richard Wright's novels to Willow: "My mother became too ill to work and I began to do chores in the neighborhood." Then show Willow how to go through her notes, make up a sentence for any topic she's nervous about, jot down a brief outline, and *memorize the outlines only.* They will serve to jog her memory, should she need them.

A final word: Please, save all your kids' test essays. Not only are they records of what they know at the moment, they're also mementos of their growth. And every teacher's mark will help you show your kids how to do better on the next test. Those marks and comments will help guide your kids to get higher grades the next time around.

Notes & Quotes

_____

_____

_____

_____

_____

Hold on: What if your time is especially short right now, and you can't work on any top teacher tips at the moment? What then? Then wait until you have some time or until your vacation. Meanwhile, just focus on testing fundamentals.

39 Prepare Well for All Tests

PARENT POINTER *Teach your kids how to study.*

If you're running a marathon, you prepare yourself. That's a given. You'll take as much as three months, six months, a year, or more to get yourself in shape physically. You'll also see to the proper diet, maybe even practice mental exercises, visualizing each step you take as you run the race.

FYI

In earlier chapters we've discussed the mechanics of studying and test-taking drills and skills. While they all help enormously, there's another often-overlooked component to consider besides the actual learning and testing strategies: your kids' general health.

HELPFUL HOW-TO HINTS

SMART STARTER Most adults do best with eight hours of sleep at night. Quickly check how many hours of sleep Jordana gets. She needs ten hours, so make sure she gets them. That's especially important before any test.

Next, check on what Jordana eats. For kids, breakfast is the most important meal because it gets them off to a great start, especially on test days. Fortunately, today there are many kid-friendly breakfast foods. So let Jordana help you plan her breakfast menu for the week. Then whip up the pancakes, waffles, or cheese toasties in advance on the weekend, so they can be microwaved in nothing flat. A delicious school lunch is also a must. To produce her best test results, Jordana needs the most nutritious diet she can get.

After that, become a couch potato grouch. That means get Jordana up and out. The sofa and TV aren't going to be her only places to chill anymore. Remember, this is a growing girl. Her muscles need exercise just like her mind, and one potentiates the other. So check Jordana's schedule: Does she get at least thirty minutes of physical exercise every day? Are the two of you out jogging every evening? Jumping rope? Playing ball?

Plan the exercise with Jordana's homework in mind. Call out her spelling words while you walk the dog together every morning. Her improving scores are your reward.

Teach Jordana to be positive by example. That means work on being cheerful yourself every day. Choose an inspiring motto for your family, such as Hemingway's "courage and confidence!" Under no circumstances burden Jordana with your lifelong fears and doubts. Those are *your* challenges to deal with, not hers. Her mind and heart need to be free: to long, learn, and leap ahead.

SUPER STARTER

Tell Jaimie to consider his tests in school like a game of football, basketball, or other sport he likes. The time to get ready is *before* the event so he won't have to put in time *afterward* worrying and agonizing.

Help him keep a record of time spent studying for all major tests and what the results are. That way he can see for himself that upping his study time will result in his exam scores going up too.

Help Jaimie distance himself from too big a dose of TV, video games, movies, and computer activities. Many of those stress second-rate values or gobble up his time mindlessly. You want him to be the best. So unless a program is educationally valuable, have Jaimie switch to the best TV of all, channel O-F-F. And set a time limit for his techno toys.

These days 20 percent of kids are emotionally not on an even keel. That means they could benefit from counseling. Observe Jaimie day to day and make a record of anything that worries you about his behavior. Can he control his temper? Is he fairly happy most of the time? If not, make sure he gets some help immediately. Kids who are chronically upset always score lower on tests than those who are at peace overall. And that's only one reason you have to seek assistance for him. Another is to keep Jaimie out of trouble.

How about you? Please, don't have a fight with your spouse the night before Jaimie's big test. If at all possible, don't move out of the home or separate during the week of his final exams. The grades of kids whose parents go through a divorce frequently plummet. But eventually—if Mom and Dad act unselfishly—those grades recover. So, please, choose a calm time in Jaimie's school year to make a major family change. Think of his progress, his success.

Consider the home atmosphere you provide for your kids. To score higher on their quizzes, kids need a solid foundation: a calm home, set routines, some financial stability, and, most important, emotional stability. And please, along with their cereal every morning, ladle out a large dose of joy.

Notes & Quotes

_____

_____

_____

_____

_____

Keep in mind always: Your kids need you. Your love and care and attention are to them what warm rays of sun and soft streams of rain are for plants. Yet your kids' wishes are quite simple. They really want nothing more than to grow up to be productive citizens and make you proud.

One special way your kids want to make you proud is to lift any burdens they cause you, financially or otherwise, off your shoulders. Help your kids with that wish. Think long range—beyond their elementary years.

TOP TIP

40 Take Trial SAT-type Tests Early

PARENT POINTER *Teach your kids to practice for life-changing tests years before taking them.*

Beyond the regular subject tests schools demand and the academic ratings that districts and states require, there are some scholastic tests that can make a huge difference in the lives of your kids. When you were in high school, those were the PSAT, SAT, and ACT tests, or College Boards, which were created to assess levels of scholastic aptitude and achievement.

Nowadays, tests like these and others are offered much earlier, beginning in fifth or sixth grade in some cases. The reason may be to select your children for advanced summer camps or accelerated school programs. Or maybe you're considering sending your child to a private school, where similar tests are the norm for admission, especially at the more demanding private schools.

FYI

Sending your kids to private school may never have crossed your mind, and you believe that worrying about your kids' high school success now is plain premature. Even fifth, sixth, seventh, or eighth grade can seem far away for parents of younger children.

OK. But consider this: Most educators suggest that you work with your kids two to three years before they ever have to face a test of the SAT's magnitude. By that they mean any scholastic achievement test, the results of which could be life-changing for your kids. To start now may not be so premature. On the contrary, this may be exactly the right time.

HELPFUL HOW-TO HINTS

SMART STARTER   Begin by thinking about your life. Is it everything you always wanted it to be from a professional standpoint? Or could you be achieving more right now if you had had a better education? Or perhaps you wish you had applied yourself more. Only you can answer these questions. Keep them in mind as you now consider your son Cooper, that dear boy who has his father's eyes, his mother's hair, and a stubborn streak that neither of you claims.

Then picture Cooper twenty years from now, all grown up and finished with his education. What kind of life do you envision for him? If you could pick his career, what would you choose? Why? Again, only you can answer these questions, but in all likelihood you want Cooper to do the kind of work that commands a healthy respect plus a healthy salary, right? Nobody wants their kids to work themselves to the bone, underpaid and disrespected.

Here comes a hard step. Think back again, way back. Was there anything you regret in the way your parents raised you? Did they support you always in your schoolwork, or were they too busy making a living? Can you list what they did to encourage you to want to make top grades? Or did they fail you academically?

Next comes an even harder step: Stop the pendulum. Generations often go from one extreme to the other when it comes to child rearing. People who had strict parents raise their kids with a nonchalant attitude: "If you want to drop out of high school, go ahead, it's your life." Predictably, the dropout will then try to make his or her own kids super-achievers, and so on. You must find the right balance between not caring about your kids' scores and living only through their school success.

You have to look at Cooper, see his potential, and give him all the study advantages you can. Then step back and feel fulfilled, not through Cooper's greatness but through the fact that you gave your best.

Now you know precisely what to do. Just raise your expectations. Know that potentially your kids can be any-thing they want to be. And then what? Take some of the following steps.

SUPER STARTER Drive to the bookstore and do some research on books about testing. Take Camille with you and let her help you buy a stack of pre-PSAT/SAT preparation materials, from printed to computer-ized versions. Then choose the easiest questions from those books or programs and let her try them. Sit at the table or PC with her and say, Let's figure this problem out together.

Later, say, Here's a brand-new notebook, Camille. Let's look at this page of tough questions (in the pre-PSAT/SAT prep book) and see how many words you don't know. Let's read this paragraph and do the same. Then copy the words, and we'll look them up together. Then we'll make up some antonyms (opposite words) and see if we're right. Want to? Camille will be only too happy to have your love and attention. Strengthen the bond between you, which in later years might become tested. By reinforcing it now, every time you have a minute, it will withstand anything that comes up the road.

On another day, see if there are any advanced scholastic programs for middle-school kids in your area, find out what it takes to get admitted to them, and pick up materials that will prepare Camille to apply later. If she likes science, see if there's a summer program in science for gifted middle-schoolers; they are often held on university campuses during the summer months. With your help now, Camille will be ready to apply for a spot when her times comes.

Don't stop here. Are there gifted and talented classes in Camille's school? Find out what it takes to get into them. Then provide Camille with the appropriate test prep materials so she can be included in the future.

And while you're exploring all the academic possibilities for Camille's future, get a curriculum guide from that private school you've heard about and compare and contrast its courses with what the public school offers. Does Camille's academic program measure up? If not, what can you do to ensure that she'll score well in comparison to the private-school students? In the years to come, it doesn't matter what elementary or middle schools your kids attended; what matters is what they learned.

Notes & Quotes

One lasting way to make your kids as smart as you can, no matter how old they are, is to make them better thinkers. You can't always be around your kids, especially as they grow older. Working on increasing your kids' ability to think for themselves is a sure way to make them smarter.

Part IX: Thinking Smarts

Help your kids to . . .
become better thinkers

"Why can't my students think?" is a common complaint from teachers all across the country. "Why can't they transfer what I taught them last week to what I'm teaching this week?" Deep sigh.

Teachers overlook an important fact when making these statements: Often our kids *do* know the material, and know it well, but they just can't apply it. So you, Mom or Dad, need to tackle that problem.

TOP TIP
41 | Enjoy Thinking

PARENT POINTER *Encourage your kids to spend time thinking.*

Being able to think clearly is an important skill that underlies all learning and is one that doesn't have a short shelf life (like diagramming a sentence or reciting the periodic table of elements). Indeed, clear thinking is the firm foundation upon which all school exercises build. It will always help us, whether we're nine or ninety.

Once your kids have this skill well developed, nothing much can set them back, for if they can think on their own, they will flourish, in school and out. Isn't it fantastic that this ability can be honed and honored, just like lesser scholastic skills?

FYI

George Bernard Shaw said he tried to think once a week, while other people never did. That's a harsh assessment of mankind. In fact, many more people do think, but often they feel guilty about it. Just sitting around and thinking makes them feel like they're wasting time, yet they're doing something that ennobles human beings.

In our busy lives, how can we get our kids to take up the habit of thinking?

HELPFUL HOW-TO HINTS

SMART STARTER Begin the process by giving Kenton *time* to think. Sit in the backyard with him one evening, just the two of you, and look up at the stars. Allow his mind to wander far and wide, as yours will.

Encourage Kenton to ask questions, any he wants at first, then more intelligent and pertinent ones. But answer all questions patiently. Don't say "I don't know," unless you add, "But I know how to find out." Then do it together. This way, you're encouraging his curiosity, not squelching it.

If Kenton asks you a question that makes you uncomfortable, track down an appropriate book for him to read. His school librarian will point you in the right direction. Before giving Kenton the book, however, read it first yourself. Better for your son to have too little information than to give him any misinformation.

Draw Kenton into lively family discussions. Ask what he thinks about a current issue and ask him to defend his opinion. Don't interrupt him. Instead, let him explain his reasons. By being willing to listen to him, you're fostering his skill to wait his turn before speaking.

Nudge him to talk about his own ideas and feelings. The more he can express himself, the more he'll be free to enjoy thinking constructively. If Kenton has no way to vent feelings like anger verbally, he may do so physically.

Teach him to think, What if . . . ? What if plants could talk? What if kids got only two weeks off from school per year? What if there were no wars?

SUPER STARTER Help Krystal to think more clearly and be able to express her thoughts by assigning her various subjects for discussion at the supper table. One evening give her a topic requiring an explanation from her (How do you pick out your school clothes?). Next comes a topic that requires an argument (The teenage years should start at age ten). She can jot down her key points and refer to them. For dessert: her favorite homemade German chocolate cake or the raspberry sherbet she craves.

On the next long ride, offer Krystal some "speech specials." Ask her to think for two minutes, then talk on some famous quotations, such as "A horse! a horse! my kingdom for a horse!" (Shakespeare, *Richard III*, V.iv.7), or "God loveth a cheerful giver" (2 Corinthians 9:7).

Next time, ask Krystal to think for a while and then introduce herself to you as if she were already the famous person she hopes to be someday. What exactly does she say?

Encourage Krystal to think critically about the hidden messages of TV shows, computer and video games, movies, magazines, and radio programs. Have her think of, and participate in, alternative activities, like sports.

Similarly, teach her to think critically about the real motives her classmates, friends, or people in general have when they try to persuade her to do something. Krystal should learn to ask herself in all situations, What would Mom and Dad want me to do here?

This question will make your kids smarter by leaps and bounds, because, of course, your kids know that you want them always to

> do their best academically
>
> have good discipline
>
> use good values
>
> set high goals
>
> think before acting

So practice this question over and over with your kids and post it in their rooms. WHAT WOULD MOM AND DAD WANT ME TO DO HERE? The answer will always be the right one.

Notes & Quotes

_____

_____

_____

_____

_____

The reason your kids need to think is because they don't grow up in a vacuum. In today's schools, especially, they're surrounded by kids from all kinds of backgrounds. Therefore, your kids may be in class or be assigned to group work not only with the kids you'd choose for them but with others as well. It can be tough for your kids to find just the right friends.

But rather than have them focus exclusively on their peers, teach your kids to become their own best friends. That means, while they continue to look for good friends, they shouldn't sit around bored, bored, bored.

Instead, they should work on being more interesting themselves and be able to think of fun and positive things to do on their own.

42 | Expand Your Thinking

PARENT POINTER *Teach your kids to broaden their thinking.*

Boredom in kids can promote bad behavior. Especially in bright kids, it can lead to many unhealthy or destructive activities, and the older bored kids get, the more damage they can do to themselves or others.

It gets worse if several bored kids band together. For whatever act of minor vandalism occurs to one kid, his or her pals are sure to top it and maybe turn a harmless prank into a really heinous act.

Worst of all, kids who get into the habit of getting their thrills out of troublemaking will do just the opposite of what you want them to: become smarter. How do you stop that trend?

FYI

Show your kids what a good friend you are to yourself by steadfastly working to overcome any detrimental habits you might have. That way, they will be proud of you and won't tune you out when you remind them of Mark Twain's epigram: "When I was fourteen, my father was so ignorant that I couldn't stand to be around him. When I got to be twenty-one, I was amazed at how much the old man had learned in seven years." Your kids will continue to emulate you and really hear you as you continue to improve their thinking abilities.

HELPFUL HOW-TO HINTS

SMART STARTER Help Benna examine the world around her and think about what's going on. Just because the latest fad is having purple hair, she doesn't have to dream of violet tresses. Same goes for those ever-shrinking tank tops.

Teach Benna to consider opposites. When she clamors for more possessions, ask her to pretend she had to give half her "stuff" away. Say, What if you could only keep three toys? Which ones would you chose? Why?

Enlist Benna in solving a problem that your family has. Problem solving is one of the best ways for her to stretch her thinking capacities. If she's begging for a Disney World vacation, have her help research how much that vacation would cost and ask her advice on how to save that much money. Is Benna willing to give up her allowance? Feed the neighbors' cats while they're on vacation and contribute any extra cash she might earn? Kick in that birthday check from Granddad?

Buy large sheets of paper, tack them up in the kitchen or den, and brainstorm together. Whatever problem Benna has, show her how to jot down any ideas, solutions, or changes she can think of. Meanwhile, call out some of your own; then take a break and get back to the brainstorm list later. Keep it posted for several days so Benna can think of more ideas.

SUPER STARTER Teach Benny the nuances and shades of words, the various ways we can look at a situation, and point out that it's rare for two people to see an event the same way. He should always be quick to think, and think hard, but be slow to judge.

Then tell Benny the old adage "We're never in the same stream twice." What does that mean? What are some of the constantly changing aspects of our lives? What are the constants, which don't change and never will?

Spend time with Benny talking about how life has changed since you were born. Then ask him to hone his prediction skills. What will be the next techno revolution? Have Benny put his prediction in writing by answering this question: What will life be like in the year 2022? Save Benny's predictions, to be read again in 2022 (by Benny and his kids).

On another day, tell Benny the beginning of a book that has changed your life or deeply inspired you. But tell him only the opening event; let him anticipate the rest of the story. Then mention the ending and have Benny suggest another one.

Discuss any incidents of crass materialism and false political promises with Benny, then have him tell you similar occurrences he's noticed. Laugh with him over the outrageous things some people try to get away with these days and ask Benny for his solutions. Give him a few days for thought and research. Then help Benny pass on his newfound knowledge or suggestions for change (via e-mail) to friends or to people in leadership positions.

Ask Benny to collect some famous quotes that have meaning for him. Ask him to memorize them as food for further thought. Teach that in thinking we have a choice: either to think of something completely new and original or to expand some idea someone else has already voiced.

Share the following two famous quotes with Benny—they can be applied to many events in our world—and use them as thought starters:

1. Let every nation know . . . that we shall pay any price, bear any burden, meet any hardship, support any friend, oppose any foe to assure the survival and the success of liberty.

—John F. Kennedy

2. This is our hope. This is the faith with which I return to the South. With this faith we will able to hew out of the mountain of despair a stone of hope.

—Dr. Martin Luther King, Jr.

Ask Benny, What events in history can be related to the first quote? To what current problems in our society do the words in the second quote speak?

Notes & Quotes

_____

_____

_____

_____

_____

Trust me: With these thought-expanding strategies you will be sure to get your kids thinking. But to keep your kids thinking even more, teach them not only to expand their thinking but also to do the opposite: to simplify.

43 | Learn to Simplify Information

PARENT POINTER *Teach your kids to make even the most difficult concepts understandable.*

When you have to put together a complicated toy for your six-year-old, don't you just love it when the dreaded words *some assembly required* come with a short illustrated chart and simple instructions saying, First do this; next, the other; and finally, that. Oh, how you appreciate accurate drawings and instructions that are right on the money. Because one-two-three, you're done!

FYI

Unfortunately, textbooks aren't that simple. Often they present your kids with slow introductions, lengthy explanations, and verbose summaries. Their tests can also go on for pages. Often the instructions alone run for many paragraphs. And it gets worse, the older your kids become.

So it's best to teach your kids how to simplify lengthy passages and quickly get to the point of whatever assignments they face, in school and in life. How do you teach that skill? Like everything else, a little at a time, but always with success in mind.

HELPFUL HOW-TO HINTS

SMART STARTER From early on, teach Aaron to sketch what he's reading. Let's assume he has this math problem to solve: You have a dozen apples, and seven friends come over. All of you want to share the apples equally. How much does each one of you get? First thing, ask him to draw 12 apples; next, 8 (7 plus 1) stick people. Draw arrows, connecting each apple with a person. Four apples remain. Teach Aaron to cut the remaining apples in half—and there's his answer: Each person gets 1½ apples.

Also introduce Aaron to simple charts and help him draw several of his own. It's great to print out a pie chart on the computer, but even better to know how to draw one by hand. To illustrate: If Aaron gets a two-dollar allowance and every week spends $1.50 on candy, show him graphically what that does to his financial holdings. Draw a pie shape and shade in three-fourths, which you label "candy." He'll understand right away where most of his money goes.

Also help Aaron make connections from his allowance pie chart to other, more complex drawings. Show him newspaper charts, stock market graphs, maps, and other illustrations, teach him how to interpret them, and have him design his own.

Give Aaron a long paragraph to read and ask him to list three key points in the paragraph. Demonstrate to him how to read carefully, underline major points, and cut through all the extra words.

Show Aaron how to add and subtract by going both from left to right (if there's a series of numbers) and from right to left. To double-check additions, take the sum and subtract the original numbers. To double-check subtractions, take the end result and add to it what was subtracted.

Also explain the concept of "guesstimation" to Aaron. Let's say he's faced with this problem:

What do you get when you add ½ and 1¼?

(a) 5   (b) 3¾   (c) ⅔   (d) 2⅔   (e) none of the above

By sketching half a pie, one whole pie, and a quarter of a pie, Aaron can tell right away that the correct answer has to fall somewhere between 1 and 2. Since answers *a* through *d* do not, only *e* is the correct choice.

SUPER STARTER Ask Arielle to pretend her mind is a Web site with many links and then ask what she learned in class today. What link exists in her mind to tie this new piece of information to something she already knows?

Play "History Links" with her. You name a date and she'll quickly give you a related topic of one or two words. To help in this, have her memorize a historical highlight for every century, then quiz you.

Ask Arielle to invent a new kids' game. Have her write out some simple rules and design a board and then play the game together. Have her check to see if there's a market for her invention.

Tell Arielle the ending of a famous play (act 3) and have her guess what acts 1 and 2 might have been.

Ask Arielle to write a seven-page math booklet for kids younger than she is. It should contain a page each on numbers, percentages, fractions, decimals, multiplication, division, and measurements. After that she'll illustrate the booklet, entitle it "The Math Path," and send it to an elementary class in a foreign country. In three weeks she might get an answer, including samples of some of their work.

Notes & Quotes

_____

_____

_____

_____

_____

All these exercises combine pleasure with thinking because they encourage your kids to engage their minds, find solutions, learn to puzzle out word problems, and, while doing so, gain confidence in their thinking. Soon your kids will be just brimming over with all kinds of sparkling ideas. At that point you will want them to have many avenues of expression. These avenues will invite your kids to keep thinking—and to keep enjoying the process.

44 Find a Way to Express Your Thoughts

PARENT POINTER *Encourage your kids to start a collection of their thoughts.*

Abstract thinking is like abstract painting: It doesn't necessarily make sense at first and it doesn't always relate to something else. It can just be free-floating, like feathery clouds in a blue sky. We may come up with our most creative thoughts this way, our best ideas, but they are indeed like the clouds—fleeting. So we write them down, not just as a testament to the past but as a wellspring for new ideas, growth, and hope in the future.

FYI

For a moment, think back over your life. Do you have a record of your most important thoughts for each year of your life? That is, not just a diary but a chronological listing that details how your thinking and your feelings evolved over the decades? How surface concerns once occupied your mind almost totally, but how, as you grew older, you learned to look beneath outer appearances to appreciate and honor real values in others and in yourself?

Of course, you can't recover those lost thoughts. But you can make sure your kids have the opportunity to express what's weighing on their minds right now. With that they can start a collection, to which they can add over the years.

HELPFUL HOW-TO HINTS

SMART STARTER Ask Carpenter to find a pretty stone, have him scrub it in the sink, dry it, and draw a face on it (with marking pens or nail polish). Then say, Make up a new name for this stone. Then tell me about Stoney's life.

Another day say, Let's send Stoney to school. What would his school be like? What would he learn? Who would his friends be? Draw the school and write a paragraph about Stoney's class.

Or, ask Carpenter for a list of adjectives describing Stoney and his family. Then write a story about Stoney's secret wish. Would he like to come alive? If so, what would he do? What would he eat? What games would he play?

Let Carpenter look around the house and tell you what each piece of furniture might say if it could talk. Then find out which of all those statements is the most interesting to Carpenter. Why?

Give Carpenter a sheet of paper, have him write down the numbers 1 through 10, and then ask him to fill in what he thinks occupied his mind most at age one, age two, age three, and so on. Post it.

Next time Carpenter has friends over, give them some old athletic socks and ask them to make people out of them. They can cut faces from magazines, glue them on the socks, and stuff them with rags. Give them a box filled with paper plates, plastic cups and spoons, Popsicle sticks, bits of ribbon, and construction paper. Soon they will build a whole city in which the

Sock folks live. Then ask them to write a play with their characters. Carpenter will be the narrator. A year later repeat the process, and notice the development of your son's ideas.

SUPER STARTER Caryn would love her own chalkboard, so buy one and ask her to write something on it every day. Every Saturday, when she cleans up her room, ask her to choose from the board the most important words or phrases of the week and record them in a notebook. Erase the rest.

Ask Caryn to read her favorite poem to you, then tell her to rewrite the poem as a short skit. Volunteer to read the skit with her, playing all the parts she assigns to you. Then ask her what she wanted you to understand from the skit. What was the message?

Give Caryn a blank journal. Ask her to write in the dates for the upcoming year and add a meaningful, encouraging, positive sentence for each day for kids her age. This is a great group project for Caryn and her friends; they can take snapshots of scenes at school. Then see if Caryn's Calendar can't become a reality with a small contribution from the PTA (or from her grandparents).

Ask Caryn to research how the concerns of kids have changed over the past century. She can interview people in the community and find out what people who were kids in the 1920s, 1930s, 1940s, and so on had uppermost on their minds. By the time Caryn gets to her decade, the present one, she might find out that the cares of kids have changed a lot over the past century. Or not. Then she can predict future concerns and record them.

Have a "great ideas" contest at your house. Keep a stack of paper slips on the kitchen counter, in the car, and on Caryn's nightstand, and tuck some in with her lunch each day. Tell her to write down any great ideas she has during the week and slip them into a suggestion box you set up. The rest of the family does likewise. Then on Saturday, during a breakfast of waffles and sausage, read the ideas, discuss and evaluate them, vote on them, save the best ones, and praise the writers.

Notes & Quotes

_____

_____

_____

_____

It doesn't have to be at breakfast, of course. It can be a lunch or a Sunday-evening supper out. But it's best to set up a weekly routine during which you can strengthen the ties of your family and acknowledge the special contributions of your kids.

Celebrating your kids becoming better thinkers is as important as celebrating their soccer team's wins or the excellent results in their school's band competition. As your kids try to figure out what's wrong with the world, which they will inevitably do as they start thinking more and more, you need to show them they don't stand alone.

Latching on to the injustices of the universe as they learn to use their minds better can make kids feel lonely. Suddenly they look beneath the obvious and wonder, Why? For that reason, kids must be taught that, in their examination of what's going on in this world, they are only the latest explorers in a long line.

45 Study World Thinkers and Their Ideas

PARENT POINTER *Teach your kids about some of the world's greatest ideas.*

One great thing about living in the twenty-first century is that so much has already been discovered and so many worthwhile ideas have already been expressed. By studying the history of mankind, we can look into the minds of the greatest thinkers of the past, pick their brains, so to speak, and then try to see beyond them. Far beyond.

FYI

That's the vision you want your kids to have. They can explore the realms of thought, dating back to the dawn of history, and, while doing so, feel a real kinship with all those who went before them: all those who took full advantage of their educational opportunities and tried their best, no matter how limited their classrooms, textbooks, or teachers were hundreds of years ago.

Some of them had no teachers. Everything they learned, they had to teach themselves. No quick computer check for them! But even after the first schoolhouse came into existence, educational facilities were vastly different from the schools of today. It wasn't until the 1960s that all kids in this country were given the chance for an equal education.

Yet long before then, the spark that is in each human being burned bright. In some people it grew into a flame that's still lighting the world today, hundreds or thousands of years after their deaths. While these extraordinary thinkers are long gone, their ideas remain. They instruct, influence, and inspire us. They are our scholastic pathfinders. Let's give your kids a chance to walk along those paths. It will humble, hearten, and hoist them up to even more thinking of their own.

HELPFUL HOW-TO HINTS

SMART STARTER Who were some of those great minds? Ask Justine if she knows a great man or woman from the past and help her research that person's greatest contribution.

Make your own short list of the world greatest thinkers and ask Justine if she's ever heard of any of them. Let her pick one or two and look them up on the Internet to see if the ideas these thinkers supported have meaning for her.

Ask Justine what she knows about the lives of the following famous women: Joan of Arc, Phillis Wheatley, Marie Curie, Sojourner Truth, and Margaret Mead. Then tell her to find out how these women were educated and what problems they had to face.

Another time, ask Justine what she considers the most awesome sight of the world. The Statue of Liberty? The Eiffel Tower? Tell her about the Seven Wonders of the World, those ancient works that people in the Greek and Roman world found most awe-inspiring. Let Justine read up on the Pyramids of Egypt, the Hanging Gardens of Babylon, and the five other wonders, then research the designers and builders of those early monuments and try to find out whose creation they were.

SUPER STARTER Ask Jeff what he knows about the religions of the world and ask him to read up on some of them. Mention Aristotle, Plato, and Socrates. Ask him who these men were and what they contributed to civilization. Can Jeff tell you and the rest of the family why these names still have so much clout today?

Sit down with Jeff and help him construct a kids' version of *Who Wants to Be a Millionaire* that includes famous philosophers and religious leaders of the past, then find out if Jeff's teacher will allow this game to be played in the classroom on a day before vacation or another appropriate time.

Ask Jeff to contact professors or librarians from a nearby university to find out whom they judge to be our greatest thinkers or leaders. Then let Jeff read biographies of these men and women.

Finally, have him condense the works of those men and women he thinks have advanced society the most into a single sentence or quote for each one. Ask him to use some of these quotes on bookmarks he'll design. In Jeff's research, he may come across outstanding economists, educators, historians, military leaders, scientists, and leaders from many other fields, including famous authors from the past. One of them is Ralph Waldo Emerson, whose epigrams (wise and witty words) include:

> The only way to have a friend is to be one.

> We boil at different degrees.

> Nothing great was ever achieved without enthusiasm.

Notes & Quotes

_____

_____

_____

_____

_____

How true, especially that last epigram. It's right on target for making your kids smarter, too, so do it with joy.

The last section of this book will show you how you can add immeasurably to your kids' brightness by giving them one more thing—the ability to appreciate the beauty of the whole world.

Part X: Art Smarts

Help your kids to . . .

love art and artistic expression

Most teachers realize how important the arts are in the lives of your kids, but too often the pressures of the curriculum prevent them from including the arts as much as they'd like to in their lesson plans. That's why it is imperative for you, Mom and Dad, to step in.

TOP TIP

46 | Love the Arts

PARENT POINTER *Take your kids to the art museum, concert hall, opera, and theater.*

The arts add a golden dimension to ordinary things and uplift your kids in uncounted ways. They increase their creativity and feed their imagination. They also bring excitement and novelty to their lives, as they train your kids' senses and let them explore their talents to the fullest. Best of all, that training and increasing creativity can pay off in increased academic achievement.

FYI

Painting, sculpture, and music are important for your kids, so
what the schools don't provide, you, of course, have to—and
want to. So make sure your children get exposed to the arts
in three ways: (1) as performers, (2) as fans, and (3) as students
of art history.

HELPFUL HOW-TO HINTS

SMART
STARTER
Ask Shepard about his favorite drawing, and
he'll show you a picture he drew last week.
Ask him about it, post it in a prominent
place, then expose him to various styles of drawing and painting. Ask, Which one do you like? If he points to portraits,
show him a picture of the Mona Lisa by Leonardo da Vinci,
and have him tell you if he likes it or not. Then let him use a
camera to take pictures of some local faces he finds interesting.

Take him to an art museum, and on the first visit let
Shepard lead you. (On later visits, have a museum guide
show both of you around and explain the significance of the
collection.) Allow Shepard to buy some postcards from the
museum gift shop and help him post a collection of them in
his room. Or have him design a collage, using the museum
postcards and his own drawings, and hang it from the ceiling.

Another time, take Shepard to an outdoor concert in your
area. Afterward ask him what selection he enjoyed most. The
two of you together can read up on other works by the composer, for example, John Philip Sousa, and buy or rent some
tapes or CDs with more selections by him or similar artists.

Encourage Shepard to sing along with the radio or with
you. Teach him the songs your parents sang. Play an instrument

with him, or find out if Shepard would like to learn to play the clarinet, for instance. Then see about some lessons for him. What does his school have to offer in the way of music education?

SUPER STARTER Encourage Shayna to draw flowers, animals, and landscapes by buying her a sketch pad, pencils, and charcoal. Then sit down and draw along with her. Exhibit Shayna's work or mail it to her favorite aunt and uncle.

Take Shayna to a bookstore and let her browse through art books until she finds a style that speaks to her. If she's interested in Impressionist paintings, plan a trip with her to a museum that has an exhibit by Renoir. Or have her write to the museum, requesting a catalog. Or visit the museum via the Internet. Also take Shayna to a local art gallery and let her experience some of the other styles of painting in vogue today. Then arrange for her to visit a local artist's studio and ask about the artist's early years.

Make sure Shayna has a chance to listen to classical music, in addition to her favorite pop CDs. Also teach her to read music and write her own simple songs. Or have her choose a favorite poem, select some appropriate background music for it, tape the music, and play the tape at low volume while she reads the poem aloud.

If possible, take Shayna to a musical and make the excursion an occasion to remember. Or rent several videos of musicals and enjoy them at home with her. Ask Shayna to invite her friends, then serve popcorn, soft drinks—the works. Later, when it's just you and Shayna again, try to outdo each other with your best rendition of Broadway tunes. Loudness is encouraged.

One day when Shayna dances through the house, say, Freeze. Then tell her about famous sculptures and have her practice some poses she thinks a sculptor would find fascinating. Talk to her about Michelangelo and Rodin and take her to see some of their amazing work. Let Shayna take a ceramics class. But before that, check to see what art classes her school has to offer.

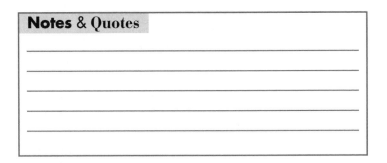

Notes & Quotes

You may feel frustrated, as you encourage your kids to become more interested in the arts, because there is such a wealth of art you want them to experience. Not only do huge numbers of great works exist in many different media in the United States today, but so also do other countries and centuries boast of innumerable priceless masterpieces. Introduce your kids to at least some of the most outstanding works and artists from various parts of the world and from different time periods.

47 | Study Famous Artists and Their Work

PARENT POINTER *Expose your kids to some of the great artists and their work.*

Nothing is more counterproductive to your kids' best school performance than a feeling of having been left out of, or behind in, the mainstream of learning. Put simply: Kids don't want to be dumb or seem to be dumb in front of their classmates.

Once they think of themselves as dumb, they start pretending to be really stupid; maybe that'll get a rise out of their fellow students whom they cannot impress by being smart. Next up for these pretend dummies: They stop caring about their schoolwork, which leads to their truly becoming less educated. In other words, in their way of thinking, they just get dumb and dumber. Why not? And the longer that process of feeling and becoming stupid persists, the greater the detrimental effect.

In the end, we find students just entering middle school who are already several years behind their classmates. This happens far too often these days. In many school systems over half of the kids in the third or fourth grade cannot pass a minimum competency test.

FYI

This pervasive "dumbing down" of our kids can be stopped. Instead of expecting less and less of our students, we must expect more and more. Counteract encroaching dumbness by encouraging smartness. Give your kids a chance to know more than what they're exposed to routinely in school. Fill in whatever academic gaps you see they have, especially in their appreciation of great art.

HELPFUL HOW-TO HINTS

SMART STARTER Think of the land in which we live and introduce Michelle to some of its early art forms. What does she know about Navajo weaving? Hopi dolls? Centuries ago, what Native American tribes lived in your state, and what is their artistic legacy? Let Michelle pull up all kinds of fascinating information on American Indian art on the Internet.

Hang up a bulletin board in the hallway and ask Michelle to decorate it with pictures of famous architectural wonders. Tell her to scout around and see what she can find on her own. She can ask her teacher and the librarian to direct her.

Ask, Michelle, do you know what jazz is? Tell her what you know about it and introduce her to the works of Edward Kennedy Ellington, otherwise known as Duke. Tell her that many great musicians are multitalented. They not only compose new music, they also play one or more instruments brilliantly, and they conduct. Another time tell her about the big-band era and let her listen to some tapes or CDs from that time.

Later, tell her about the Taj Mahal (Agra, India), the Sistine Chapel (Rome), and the Leaning Tower of Pisa (Italy). Turn her into an "archi-detective" and ask her to track down pictures and histories of these buildings. Then have her draw and design a temple, tower, or skyscraper she'd like to build sometime.

On a rainy day, take Michelle to a paint store and let her pick up some color strips, small sample bands on which many shades and hues of color appear. Stop by a fabric store and teach her to ask for free fabric swatches. Introduce her to abstract art and cubism; tell her what you know about Pablo Picasso and together get more background on this great artist and his body of work. Then ask Michelle to create her own abstract art with the cloth pieces and paint strips, which she can cut up.

SUPER STARTER Discuss art in general with Morton. Tell him that no matter what the form, art is always interested in pulling us in emotionally. So art, in all its many facets, must be respected. Great artists, like great athletes, represent the best talents of their nation. Then ask Morton what his favorite art form is: playing an instrument, photography, pottery, painting? Let him tell you and why.

If it's photography, introduce him to the works of Ansel Adams, then hand him a camera and some black-and-white film and say, Pretend you're scouting out the best location for a movie about kids your age. Take a dozen snapshots around the neighborhood that capture the feeling you might want to portray. Off he goes; you supervise.

If Morton has some rock bands he admires, ask him to a musical duel. He gets to play a selection by his favorite group; you play one you like; then discuss your tastes. Play a selection from an opera. Can Morton find anything appealing in this selection? Can he develop an appreciation for the composer? Can he tell you a story that would make a great opera?

Let Morton choose several countries other than his own and research what music those countries are famous for. What does the term "classical music" mean for people in Russia? Japan? China? Maybe Morton can e-mail the music departments at universities in Moscow, Tokyo, and Beijing and interview some professors or graduate students.

On a weekend, type up a chart for Morton on which he will list five famous musicians, composers, painters, sculptors, actors, architects, or photographers. Have him fill in their dates and a little about their work, depending on what he knows, and research the rest. Then ask Morton to quiz you on what he found. It's great for kids to know more than their moms and dads, which of course will encourage you to do a little extra research yourself.

Finally, use the word *surreal* next time you talk to Morton and then ask him to find out where that word came from (*surrealism*). Tell him to read up on the French poet André Breton and find out how this literary and artistic movement spread. What painters picked up the surrealistic style?

In further discussions, ask Morton what sight in nature has most impressed him so far. Was it the Pacific Ocean? Grandfather Mountain, North Carolina? The deer he saw in the woods last week? Have him get to know the most famous seascape, landscape, and animal artists of the world. Were they, in their youth, similarly impressed by the outdoors and nature?

Notes & Quotes

_____

_____

_____

_____

_____

Why did Monet spend so much time painting flowers? Like all questions, this one will lead to more introspection and thought, which is exactly what you want. You want your kids' minds to wander. You want to encourage them to wonder.

Where to next? Around the world and through many centuries in a few minutes. Fasten your seat belt. Your kids need to see the bigger picture, rather than just specialize in one art form or develop a liking for only one style.

48 Get an Overview of Art

PARENT POINTER *Teach your kids to connect art movements to historical events.*

To be able to make connections between the passing of time and art is most useful. Then, when any century is mentioned in history class, your kids can already picture a highlight or two of those hundred years in their mind's eye. They will also already be curious about what else went on during that time.

FYI

If you can give your kids just a rough outline of some of the major events in history and their accompanying ripples in the art world, they will feel confident in any class discussion. They might not know a specific work of art or a specific event, but they will have enough background to blend new knowledge with what they already know. Connected facts and figures are easier to remember than data in a vacuum. Give them a basic underlying framework, beginning now.

HELPFUL HOW-TO HINTS

SMART STARTER Take a sheet of paper and ask Etan to draw a straight line across the long way, divide the line into twenty-one equal segments, and label each segment with a number starting with 1. The segments represent all the centuries C.E., which means in a specific year in the Common Era (after the birth of Christ). Then ask Etan to look at the time line and mark down the present year. If he doesn't know how, help him find it (in segment 21). Have him draw two little stick people there, one for him, one for you.

Then ask Etan to name some famous dates, such as 1492 (Christopher Columbus reached the new world), 1607 (Jamestown, the first English colony, was established in America), and 1914 (World War I started). Let him fill them in on the time line, then explain that much has changed over the years. Can Etan name some changes, for instance, in hair and clothing styles?

Etan will wonder, How do we know? since there was no photography before the nineteenth century. Simple, you say. If you show him pictures of classical art from ancient Greece and Rome—for instance, the Discus Thrower—Etan can point out to you that today's athletes look and dress quite differently.

Next get out a world map and explain how each nation has developed certain forms of art more than others over the centuries: ceremonial masks come from Africa, silk scrolls from China, intricate landscape gardens from Japan. Sitar music represents India; brass bands, Bavaria; steel drums, the Caribbean. What does Etan think is a major American art form? He may mention movies or modern music, so ask him for his list of nominees for the Greatest Movie Ever and Greatest Song Ever. Watch Etan's favorite movie with him and listen to his favorite song. Then show him a *Lassie* rerun and play a selection from Handel's *Messiah*.

SUPER STARTER Ellie's time line will be more complex. She can draw pictures of what she envisions the following historical events might have looked like:

> 1211: Genghis Khan invades China and builds a megaempire
>
> 1324: The Aztecs found their capital city
>
> 1455: The first Bible is printed

Help Ellie find artistic depictions of these events in an encyclopedia and compare them with her drawings. Discuss her findings with her and show her how to find out more.

Have Ellie make a list of some of the periods in Western music and art from the various centuries and help her find works or artists representative of those periods. For example:

> Gothic art (cathedrals)
>
> Baroque music (Johann Sebastian Bach)
>
> Romantic music (Chopin)

Refer Ellie to her time line and ask her to choose a favorite century, then pick a country and try to find out what that country's artistic efforts were during that time. Help her visit the Web site of that country's biggest museum and see if she can view examples of their native art.

Take Ellie to a modern ballet and let her study the history of dance through books or by interviewing a professional dancer with the help of e-mail. Or she might want to visit a dance school nearby and gather information on the development of dance over the centuries. She might even choreograph (design) her own dance, incorporating a few steps or tunes popular in countries as diverse as Nicaragua and Namibia.

Notes & Quotes

_____

_____

_____

_____

_____

All this is just a springboard to more studying and thinking about the contributions made by some of the world's greatest artists of the past and present.

Now the future awaits, and the future is your kids. That's why you praise them for their increasing interest in the arts.

TOP TIP

49 Develop Your Own Talents and Interests

PARENT POINTER *Help your kids develop their own talents.*

Now is the time to examine what your kids' school offers in the way of a fine-arts program. Are there enough classes in music, band, art, and dance? Are there prints of masterpieces hanging on every classroom wall? Are murals painted on hallway and cafeteria walls? Is classical music played over the intercom in the lunchroom at least some of the time, to alternate with what kids prefer to hear if left to their own devices? Are the arts integrated into the curriculum so that each unit in literature incorporates some art and music?

What do the art studio, band room, drama room, and dance studio look like? Are they bright and modern, or are they former storage rooms furnished with nothing but discarded desks?

Are the art and music teachers certified to teach their subjects, or are they harried folks just drafted to the job? Are visiting artists a vital part of the curriculum? What assemblies devoted to the arts are scheduled throughout the school year? How much money is spent on art and music textbooks, materials, and supplies?

FYI

Even if the overall art program at your kids' school is dismal, encourage them to take an art class. Maybe, with the help of the PTA or other groups, you can donate or upgrade the equipment.

What if your kids' schedules are already jam-packed with all the required courses? Then see if there are after-school clubs they can join or form. Or maybe you can arrange for a class after school. Often art students at the local university are thrilled to tutor a youngster. A retired music teacher also might enjoy taking on pupils. Or you can guide your kids yourself as they explore their talents at home and on weekends. To have a blueprint, just set up a conference with the art or music teacher at your kids' school (or anywhere in the school system) and ask them for a course description. Then include some of what's listed in the course description in an independent home-study course with your kids.

Hey! That's home schooling them, you say. No, it's home tooling them. You're just adding to what your kids need.

HELPFUL HOW-TO HINTS

SMART STARTER Keep a small notebook from kindergarten on in which you record all observations you make about Kyson's talents. Does he like to draw? Make things out of modeling clay? Play with an Etch-A-Sketch? If so, build on these early interests and buy him drawing paper, coloring pencils (the plain and fancy types), watercolors, an easel, and clay. Set aside a corner in his room for his work, or give him space on a shelf for his colored-paper constructions.

Listen carefully to what Kyson's teachers tell you over the years. Have they noticed his special interest in music? His desire to play the drums? How he's itching to get his hands on a musical keyboard? List those teacher comments, add to them, and, when the opportunity presents itself, ask Kyson if he'd like to learn to play an instrument.

Check his notebook and see what his doodling looks like. Is he drawing cartoons or designs for his own brand of athletic shoes in his free moments? Is there an art school nearby Kyson can visit to see for himself the vast variety of courses offered?

Is Kyson interested in drafting or architecture? Find out by asking him to draw his dream house or design a new city. Or have him sketch out a bookcase he wants you to help him make for his room. Later, maybe he can visit the offices of an architect and find out what's going on.

Once a month take an especially good look at Kyson and ask him what new interests he has developed. Younger kids change their minds often. That's part of growing, part of getting smarter: to explore the talents we have, discard those we lose interest in, and zoom in on others that seem to stick with us over the years.

SUPER STARTER Take Kylee to an art supply store, tell her how much she can spend, and then watch as she selects canvas, brushes, paints. Stand back and see where her heart leads her. Later comes the hard part—finding an empty corner in your home that she can turn into her studio.

If Kylee likes clothes, show her how to add pizzazz to her old T-shirts with appliqués or velvet ribbons. Or have her draw a favorite flower or animal motif and help her transfer that motif to a T-shirt with the help of tracing paper. Buy her some colorful yarn and a big needle and show her the basic backstitch. Or get her some brilliant permanent marking pens and let her go to work.

Another time, show Kylee how to decorate plain wooden frames with fabric bits and glue, or help her make frames for her paintings from scratch. Encourage her to design a border for the walls of her room, then transfer the design to a piece of plywood, cut out a pattern, and stencil it on her walls.

Have Kylee join a community kids' choir. Or have her and three friends form their own group, and allow them to practice at your house. That may take nerves of steel and cotton in your ears. Could the practice sessions rotate from home to home?

Does Kylee's school have an annual talent show? If so, encourage Kylee to practice her trumpet solo for that event. She could compose a song of her own and have a classmate sing it, while another accompanies her on the guitar. Ask the principal if an art show can be held at the same time. The art show shouldn't only showcase your kids' and the other students' best work but also the teachers' and administrators' talents. Schools that create a community of learners and creators often find their test scores going up and up.

Notes & Quotes

_____

_____

_____

_____

_____

_____

Parents who keep encouraging their kids to experiment with the arts (not with cigarettes and drugs) soon find their kids are more confident and more interested in school. As a result, their grades climb. So, as much as possible, encourage your kids to explore their talents.

Of course, that goes for *all* the talents your kids have, be they in athletics, computers, speaking, leadership, or any other area. Kids whose talents are recognized and allowed to flourish always perform better in school. It's as if one bright light in their lives illuminates another, and the fire inside grows and becomes a passion.

But how do you imbue your kids with a passion? Especially if you don't have much time to spare, or extra money, or a spare corner for an art studio, to say nothing of the calm nerves and patience that kids' bands require? You don't have to have any of those.

There is one simple passion all kids can develop: the passion for language.

It's cost-free and easy to acquire, and its benefits are immediate as well as long-range. This passion is a guaranteed best school tool and an instant mind maximizer for kids. It hones your kids' language skills and increases their facility, and increasing your kids' facility with language increases their facility with every other school subject.

50 | Learn to Write Creatively

PARENT POINTER *Teach your kids to enjoy creative writing.*

Creative writing includes poetry, plays, short stories, novels, and movie scripts, but the easiest type of creative writing to encourage in your kids is poetry. Poetry is great literature reduced to its essence. In the field of language, it's the most accessible and yet most simplified great achievement of our civilization. If your kids can learn to love and labor over poetry, they can get smarter in big increments.

FYI

The language of poetry is everyday language that has been "heightened," intensified, reduced to its bare bones. An example is this line by William Carlos Williams: "The wise trees stand sleeping in the cold."

Doesn't that line bring to mind a dreary winter scene with snow or sleet, low-hanging gray clouds, frozen ponds, and air so icy it hurts your lungs—and in only eight words? Yet that's only the beginning. For doesn't the line also tell us about the laws of nature? The trees have seen generation after generation, have watched people, with all their foibles, come and go. That's why the trees are wise. And doesn't the line also offer hope? After sleep will come an awakening (spring).

After the cold will come warmth. And after an absence of love, perhaps love may come or return.

Amazing what a few well-chosen words can do, how they can make you think.

HELPFUL HOW-TO HINTS

SMART STARTER Explain to Britney that poetry is the work of poets, writers who describe beauty, emotion, events, or stories with an especially artistic touch. Then ask her: Tell me about a time when you were really happy. After she's told you about the day she got her dog, Peppers, ask her, Wouldn't it be great if you could take a quick snapshot of that happy feeling and pull it out any time you're not so happy? Well, that's what a poem is, a snapshot of happiness or other feelings.

Give Britney a book of poems and ask her to pick out one she likes, read it to you, and tell you why she likes it. Then ask her to write down words describing how she felt when Peppers first entered her life. Then say, Read those words to Peppers for approval and we'll post them on the fridge.

Another time, sit down with Britney and show her how to recognize two basic poetic terms, such as *rhyme* and *free verse*.

Explain rhyme first: Rhyme is the repetition of same or similar sounds and is frequently used in traditional poetry. For example:

The Swan and the Goose

A rich man bought a Swan and Goose.
One for song. The other for use.
But sad to say, his simple cook
One night the Swan for Goose mistook.

Yet in the dark about to chop
The Swan's neck right above the crop
He heard a pretty note and stayed
The whacking of the deadly blade.
Thus we can see a proper song
Is very rarely ever wrong.

—AESOP

Afterward, ask Britney, How many different end sounds are in this poem? (Five.) Which rhyming words are not spelled similarly? (Goose/use; stayed/blade.) Then explain to her that we call rhyme found at the end of a line *end rhyme* and when we find a definite pattern of rhyme we call it a *rhyme scheme.* To map out the rhyme scheme of a poem, we call the first rhyme sound *a* and the second one *b,* and so on. Therefore, the rhyme scheme for "The Swan and the Goose" is *a a b b c c d d e e.* Of course, more complicated rhyme schemes are possible.

Another time, mention to Britney that many modern poets find rhyme too restrictive. They want their words to flow naturally in whatever direction suits them and not be hampered by rules and regulations. For that reason, they prefer *free verse.* Free verse is poetry without any set pattern of rhyme or rhythm or line length.

Here is an example of free verse:

Driving to the beach one day
I stopped in a small town,
Went window-shopping in a forlorn strip mall
Just to prolong the anticipation.

This poem has no end rhyme or set rhyme scheme. Therefore, it's free verse.

SUPER STARTER Ask Brooks to choose any short traditional poem that appeals to him and memorize it. "The Swan and the Goose" is easy. Then have him chart the rhyme scheme.

Next, ask Brooks, Can you write your own poem with the rhyme scheme: *a b c a b c d d* ?

Example:

> *A well-mannered field mouse*
> *Set out one glorious day*
> *To drop in on his friend, a mole.*
> *He kept looking for the house*
> *Under piles of straw and hay*
> *When he fell into a deep hole.*
> *"Hey! Just a minute," the mole, still in pj's, said.*
> *"Next time knock, OK? So I can get out of bed."*

Finally, ask Brooks, Can you write a poem of your own in free verse? A good way to begin is with

> *Yesterday on my way*
> *to school I . . .*

Another day, suggest to Brooks that he write a ballad or a science-fiction or adventure story. Or a commercial, or the lyrics to a song. Tell him about something you wrote in school that you still remember. Better yet, how about something you thought of yesterday that you wish you had the time to write down?

Still better, let Brooks write whatever he wants to and encourage him to keep at it. Maybe once a week he can polish some of his thoughts and give them shape and form. Make a poem out of them. He can show the poems to you or not; that's his decision. After all, he's the boss in this, so let him enjoy the process. Let him skim along from thought to thought any time he wants to, jot down any ideas that crop into his head. Let him dig deep into his mind and heart, look for important ideas, search for answers. Let him develop a freedom and a feeling for words, a love of "getting it all out." Let him develop a passion for just the right phrase. And as he puts down his thoughts, watch him grow and strive to be the best student he can become. One thing for sure: Wrestling with poetry will teach him more about himself than what he knew before he started.

Notes & Quotes

_____

_____

_____

_____

That completes the fifty top teacher tips. Of all of them, which _one_ is most important to make our kids smarter? If, in our very busy lives, we can implement only one skill or drill, which one should moms, dads, caregivers, and teachers really choose?

That's easy. It's the bonus tip discussed in the next chapter: See to your kids' hearts.

All those academic skills we've discussed so far and all the school tools we've outlined will _not_ make your kids smarter in the most important area: deep inside, in their hearts. No matter how many academic hoops you put your kids through, they won't become all they can be unless you give them one last superb stroke of parenting paint, the most glorious gift we can give any human being.

Part XI: Heart Smarts

Help your kids to . . .
become really good kids

Having discussed the ten vitally important sections of smarts that top teachers want all their students to have, we must now add one more. This is the one without which all the others have no meaning, because while the others make our kids scholastically smarter, being scholastically smarter by itself doesn't cut it. Never has, never will. What's needed is not just being school smart but also to have a *heart*.

Inner smartness, inner beauty, the content of their character—kindness, honesty, honor, knowing and doing the right thing at all times—that's what the last skill and drill focuses on. Your kids must be not only smarter but better too.

What makes human beings so amazing is their ability to improve in so many ways and to contribute so much to society. We have all heard or seen examples of the utmost in human courage and unselfishness, honesty, faith, and devotion. We know the greatest quality a person can have is high morality, a strong value system, a conviction that goodness matters, honor counts, virtue rules, sacrifice endures. It's what lies in our hearts that reigns.

What a perfect opportunity you have now to check that this inner framework of good values is in place and strong in your kids.

Be a Good Kid

PARENT POINTER *Teach your kids to have
strong values.*

We adults are the guardians of the future. We shape the future
world as the past shaped us. And each and every day we set
the tone for the present. That's most crucial for families, especially those with young children. They look to us every day
for examples of how to live well, and better than we did.

FYI

We must always set a good example for our kids. Before we
make decisions, we must picture the eyes of our children on
us and ask ourselves, What would my kids want me to do
here?

Surely we don't want to cause them shame and pain. This
would condemn them to a life less perfect than it could have
been. We might even force them to spend all their years trying to creep out from under the dark shadows we threw over
them. If we stain the family name, they will be too busy trying to scrub it clean again to have time left to pursue their
own lives to their fullest extent.

So step number one in making your kids smarter not only
in brain but in heart is to live right yourself. Whether you
work as a corporate leader or a car loaner, whether you're a

porter or a politician, try to be the best person you can. That will impress your kids more than all your paychecks, perks, power, and portfolios. Kids are great copycats. They ape you because they adore you. You are their idol, so act like one. When you, by your example, show how to make the right choices, they will too—or try to.

That makes their lives so easy. They don't have to be little grown-ups at age ten. They don't have to figure out what's right or wrong every day. Either they will know instinctively or they'll know they can ask and depend on you to show them.

When your kids are doing the right thing, they won't have extra worries. They can devote themselves to the number one task of being the best students they can be. If, instead, your kids are loaded down with adult concerns, or feeling guilty because they're doing wrong, guilt and shame become huge albatrosses around their necks.

All wrongs weigh heavily and limit your kids severely. To make your kids truly smarter, free them from the chains of doing the wrong thing.

HELPFUL HOW-TO HINTS

SMART STARTER Take Joshua to a church, synagogue, mosque—in short, to a house of worship where he can get some religious training. Get him involved with a youth group there. That will help him find good friends, and he'll become a better kid if he has a chance to get involved in spiritual activities.

Have clear rules for Joshua and see that he sticks to them. That includes his basic habits and the chores he does around the house. It also includes good manners and discipline. Post the rules and praise him often. If he slips up, give him a chance to make good.

Have in place a clear set of consequences and follow through with them. Kids crave structure and consistency. They may act as if they resent a clear framework, but that's only proof of their growing pains. Behind your back, they brag about having strict parents; they know it means you really love them. Kids hate having admit to one another, Hey, my parents don't care.

Make sure Joshua can always come to you with his fears and worries. You don't ever want him to bottle up his anger and turn into a chronically upset kid. That might mean he could be consumed with rage. If you let him talk it out, he'll calm down and become violence-proof.

Also, insist on standards: Don't let Joshua be exposed to sleaze, whether it's on TV, the Internet, in videos, or in movies. Would you allow someone to pour a handful of dirt into your coffee every day? Why let your kids' minds and hearts be contaminated by certain mass media? Just say no— to trash and to poison.

SUPER STARTER Every chance you get, talk about character with Jessica. Encourage her to be modest, unselfish, and grateful. That means she should know that there's always more to be learned, that others have rights and feelings too, that we must respect all people, and that she needs to appreciate what she's got and give thanks.

From early on, encourage Jessica to volunteer. Volunteering means sharing and caring. Kids feel great when they're allowed to participate in projects that benefit others. Donate an hour a week to visiting the elderly and take Jessica along to read to folks with diminished sight. Offer your help at Jessica's school. She may not want you to tutor in her classroom, but she'll be proud that you've joined the beautification committee or set up displays in the library.

Or pick a child-care facility that looks after underprivileged kids. Then Jessica can write an inspiring "name poem" for the kids—the first letter of each line spells their name—get creative with type fonts and styles, and print out a poem for each child. Frame it and present it as a birthday gift.

Talk to Jessica about your own growing up and the pressures you faced. Point out any wrong choices you made and help her make the right ones. Talk about your own temptations and how you overcame them. Make her strong, so she can resist bad influences. Teach her to say, No, can't do it, won't work, no way. My mom and dad will kill me, take my allowance away, ground me, like, forever. Encourage Jess to read stories about heroines and heroes and discuss them with you. Mention current events and point out any better choices people in the news could've made.

Keep a running list of rewards for Jessica. That includes an allowance, plus extra cash she can earn for tougher jobs. Surprise her with a special treat once in a while. When Jess asks, What's that for? Tell her, That's because I can tell you're trying hard. And that makes me so proud of you.

If it's hard to tell Jessica how much you love her because she's let you down in the past, write her a note. Buy a blank card and draw on it, smiling to yourself. Illustrate the card, and give it to her. Focus on the future and on giving Jess every chance to do better. Also express your thanks to her teachers for helping her improve. The more you bond with her teachers, the more they will reinforce the good qualities you're encouraging at home.

Most of all, teach Jessica to pray. When she's younger, you may guide her with a favorite prayer of yours, but let her add her own words. Let her take some moments every morning and evening to express her grateful attitude and gain strength from knowing she's part of a greater plan. The lifeline she gets from praying is a million times stronger than any man-made material.

Notes & Quotes

_____

_____

_____

_____

_____

_____

We only live once. During that time we're supposed to climb our ladder and help others up too, right? That doesn't just mean to become a financial success. Ladders exist in everything we undertake. It can be a climb toward excellent health and a lovely home, toward expressing our artistic talents, toward beginning a new movement to improve mankind.

It can be a ladder of service to others or a ladder toward inner growth—how to become more spiritual, more in tune with what sets us apart from the animal world. Most important, the ladder offers rungs for us to climb up toward becoming *better* people: less selfish, less greedy, less egocentric, and more giving, helpful, accepting, open-minded, kind. Become a better person and help those around you in the process.

> *We don't live to grab and get,*
> *acquire and act on base desire.*
> *We live to understand,*
> *lend a hand,*
> *band with others,*
> *to make the world better.*

So discuss the *true* meaning of life with your kids. Discuss the exquisite beauty that resides in all of mankind. Thus every day you make them smarter and better and more what our Creator means us to become.

Epilogue

My parents are and were my heroes.

—MICHAEL JORDAN

THINK OF THE few precious years you have your kids at home. At most, you have about twenty years to work with them. Use those two decades. They're your only chance. They're your once-in-a-lifetime opportunity to ensure that the next generation becomes another great generation, greater than ever before. Be the starter to make them smarter.

Love your kids, lead them, and help them to grow up healthy and become productive citizens. Accept them for what they are—your crowning achievement, though not yet developed to their full potential.

To become fine young people, they need to do well in school. Help them to do that. Even if you choose only one skill out of all those mentioned in this book, if you make use of only one school tool, your kids will benefit.

Think of a garden. If you only plant one new thing this year, it's going to be an improvement, right? Same with your kids. Improve their skills in one single academic subject. Make them enjoy learning, and they'll want to learn more.

The other day a father asked me what I was working on, and I told him about this book. Too bad it's too late for my kids, he said.

Why? I asked.

Because they've already gotten so many bad study habits.

And? I asked.

And nothing, he said sadly. There's nothing I can do now.

Hold it, there's always something, I countered. I didn't even learn to speak English until I was twenty-one.

So you see, there's always something you can do to encourage your kids to become smarter. And each time you try, your kids profit. Remember that upward spiral I told you about, that from one school skill others spill? That kids who get turned on to reading one book soon will devour two, three, four, or more? Each improved skill is a brain building block, and one placed upon the other makes your kids' knowledge grow.

Think of the promise in your kids and how you're making sure that promise is fulfilled. In this era of dumbing down our youth, you're taking a stand. You're reversing the dumb-down trend. You're a warrior, fighting the pervasive lowering of intelligence in our nation's young with every top teacher tip you use. You're fighting back ignorance. Beating back stupidity. Thank you for everything you do on your kids' behalf to make them really and truly great.

> *Be not afraid of greatness:*
> *some are born great,*
> *some achieve greatness,*
> *and some have greatness thrust upon them.*
>
> —SHAKESPEARE, *Twelfth Night*

And some—those very lucky ones—have parents like you! Congratulations.

Appendix A: Support Systems and Organizations

PTO Today Online (Parent–Teacher Organization)

http://www.ptotoday.com/index.html
PTO Today
Circulation
2 Celinda Drive
Franklin, MA 02038

Founded in the spring of 1999, PTO Today, Inc., has quickly established itself in the center of the parent group world as a valuable resource for parents.

PTA (Parent–Teacher Association)

http://www.pta.org
National PTA Headquarters
330 North Wabash Avenue, Suite 2100
Chicago, IL 60611
Phone: (800) 307-4782
Fax: (312) 670-6783

National PTA is the largest volunteer child–advocacy organization in the United States. A not-for-profit association of parents, educators, students, and other citizens active in their schools and communities, PTA is a leader in reminding our nation of its obligations to children.

Learning First Alliance

http://www.learningfirst.org/
1001 Connecticut Avenue NW, Suite 335
Washington, DC 20036
Phone: (202) 296-5220
Fax: (202) 296-3256

The Learning First Alliance is a permanent partnership of
twelve leading educational associations that have come
together to improve student learning in America's public
elementary and secondary schools.

MegaSkills® Education Center

http://www.megaskillshsi.org/Default.htm
The Home and School Institute
1500 Massachusetts Avenue, NW
Washington, DC 20005

The MegaSkills® Education Center is devoted to academic
development and character education.

The National Coalition for Parent Involvement in Education (NCPIE)

http://www.ncpie.org/
3929 Old Lee Highway, Suite 91-A
Fairfax, VA 22030-2401
Phone: (703) 359-8973
Fax: (703) 359-0972

NCPIE's mission is to advocate the involvement of parents and
families in education and to foster relationships between home,
school, and community to enhance education.

Project Parents, Inc.

http://www.projectparents.org
46 Beach Street, Suite 502
Boston, MA 02111
Phone: (617) 451–0360

Project Parents offers workshops on several topics, including helping children become better readers.

The Partnership for Family Involvement in Education (PFIE)

http://pfie.ed.gov/
U.S. Department of Education
400 Maryland Avenue SW
Washington, DC 20202-8173
e-mail: partner@ed.gov

PFIE gives its mission as "to increase opportunities for families to be more involved in their children's learning at school and at home and to use family-school-community partnerships to strengthen schools and improve student achievement."

Appendix B: Recommended Reading

Armstrong, Thomas. *Awakening Your Child's Natural Genius: Enhancing Curiosity, Creativity, and Learning Ability*. New York: Putnam Publishing Group, 1991.

———. *In Their Own Way: Discovering and Encouraging Your Child's Personal Learning Style*. New York: Putnam Publishing Group, 2000.

———. *Seven Kinds of Smart: Identifying and Developing Your Many Intelligences*. New York: E. P. Dutton, 1993.

Bickart, Toni S., Dianne Trister Dodge, and Judy Jablon. *What Every Parent Needs to Know About 1st, 2nd and 3rd Grades: An Essential Guide to Your Child's Education*. Naperville, Ill.: Sourcebooks Trade, 1997.

Canter, Lee. *Homework Without Tears: A Parent's Guide for Motivating Children to Do Homework and to Succeed in School*. New York: HarperCollins Publishers, 1993.

Clark, Rosemarie, et al. *The School-Savvy Parent: 365 Insider Tips to Help You Help Your Child*. Minneapolis: Free Spirit Publishing, 1999.

Diamond, Marian, and Janet L. Hopson. *Magic Trees of the Mind: How to Nurture Your Child's Intelligence, Creativity, and Healthy Emotions from Birth Through Adolescence*. New York: Penguin USA, 1999.

Fujawa, Judy. *(Almost) Everything You Need to Know About Early Childhood Education: A Book of Lists for Teachers and Parents.* Beltsville, Md.: Gryphon House, 1998.

Getman, G. N. *How to Develop Your Child's Intelligence: More Successful Adulthood by Providing More Adequate Childhood.* Santa Ana, Calif.: Optometric Extension Program Foundation, 1993.

Holt, John Caldwell. *Learning All the Time.* New York: Perseus Press, 1990.

James, Elizabeth, and Carol Barkin. *How to Be School Smart: Super Study Skills.* New York: Beech Tree Books, 1998.

Johnson, Annmae. *Parents Can Teach Successfully: A Guide to Help Parents Teach Their Elementary-Age Children.* Lakeville, Minn.: Galde Press, 1998.

Luckie, William R., and Wood Smethhurst. *Study Power: Study Skills to Improve Your Learning and Your Grades.* Cambridge, Mass.: Brookline Books, 1997.

Markova, Dawna, et al. *How Your Child Is Smart: A Life-Changing Approach to Learning.* Berkeley, Calif.: Conari Press, 1992.

Peters, Ruth. *Overcoming Underachieving: A Simple Plan to Boost Your Kids' Grades and End the Homework Hassles.* New York: Broadway Books, 2000.

Phipps, Patricia A. *Multiple Intelligence in the Early Childhood Classroom.* New York: SRA (Science Research Associates), 1997.

Poretta, Vicki, et al. *Mom's Guide to Raising a Good Student.* New York: Hungry Minds, 1997.

Robinson, Adam. *What Smart Students Know: Maximum Grades, Optimum Learning, Minimum Time.* New York: Crown Publishing Group, 1993.

Schank, Roger C. *Coloring Outside the Lines: Raising a Smarter Kid by Breaking All the Rules.* New York: HarperCollins Publishers, 2000.

Sobut, Mary A., and Bonnie Neuman Bogen. *Complete Early Childhood Curriculum Resource: Success-Oriented Learning Experiences for All Children.* New York: Center for Applied Research in Education, 1991.

Stipek, Deborah, and Kathy Seal. *Motivated Minds: Raising Children to Love Learning.* New York: Owl Books, 2001.

Tuttle, Cheryl Gerson. *Thinking Games to Play With Your Child: Easy Ways to Develop Creative and Critical Thinking Skills.* Lincolnwood, Ill.: Lowell House, 1997.

Whitney, Brooks, and Tracy McGuinness. *School Smarts: All the Right Answers to Homework, Teachers, Popularity, and More!* Middleton, Wis.: Pleasant Company Publications, 2000.

Willis, Mariaemma, and Victoria Kindle-Hodson. *Discover Your Child's Learning Style: Children Learn in Unique Ways—Here's the Key to Every Child's Learning Success.* Roseville, Calif.: Prima Publishing, 1999.

Appendix C: Helpful Internet Sites

http://childparenting.about.com/parenting/childparenting/
library/weekly/topicsub3.htm

A guide to elementary-education enrichment articles found on
about.com.

http://atozteacherstuff.com/articles/getinvolved.shtml

Advice on how parents can help children do better in school.

http://www.familyeducation.com/

The Learning Network's parent channel. Many links for
parents and educators, some with grade-specific advice.

http://www.ipl.org/cgi-bin/youth/youth.out.pl?sub=
tcn0000

The Teachers and Parents' Corner, where resources for parents
and teachers from each section of the Internet Public Library
Youth Division are gathered for easy reference.

http://family.go.com/features/family_1998_04/dela/
dela48smart/dela48smart.html

Family.com's article on fostering a child's unique intelligence.

http://npin.org/index.html

> Web site of the National Parent Information Network. Of
> themselves, they say: "The mission of NPIN is to provide
> access to research-based information about the process of
> parenting and about family involvement in education. We
> believe that well-informed families are likely to make good
> decisions about raising and educating their children."

http://www.kidport.com/

> Kidport says of itself: "Kidport is an Internet-based educational
> service designed to help K–8 students excel in school. It
> provides a unique multi-step program to create empowered
> learners, not simply good students."

http://www.syvum.com/

> This site has many interactive learning tools and some software
> you may download.

http://www.superkids.com/

> This site has reviews of various software programs.

http://www.croton.com/allpie/

> Web site of the Alliance for Parental Involvement in Education

http://www.childrenspartnership.org/prnt/prnt.html

> The Children's Partnership's on-line resources for parents.

http://www.eduhound.com/

> This site has many links to education-related Web sites,
> including sites offering instruction on making your own Web
> page.

http://ericeece.org/
> The Educational Resources Information Center's clearinghouse on elementary and early childhood education.

http://www.par-inst.com/resources/default.htm
> On-line resources for parent involvement from The Parent Institute.

http://www.nagc.org/Publications/Parenting/index.html
> Highlights from *Parenting for High Potential*, the magazine of the National Association for Gifted Children.

http://www.websmartkids.org/
> A site for parents to learn how to help their children use the Internet safely and productively.

http://www.scholastic.com
> Many ideas for study and for entertaining/learning activities.

Acknowledgments

A special thank-you to Bettina Grahek and Jim Jackson, both award-winning educators, who offered valuable advice.

And to Rebecca Carpenter of www.rebeccaworks.com for her Internet research and computer expertise.

With special thanks to June Clark, my inspiring agent; to Christine Shillig, vice president and editorial director, Andrews McMeel Publishing, whose vision is extraordinary; and to Erin Friedrich, assistant editor, whose determination, dedication, and deft editing made the vision a reality.